# BRIGHT NOTES

# CRIME AND PUNISHMENT BY FYODOR DOSTOEVSKY

## Intelligent Education

INFLUENCE PUBLISHERS

Nashville, Tennessee

BRIGHT NOTES: Crime and Punishment

www.BrightNotes.com

No part of this publication may be used or reproduced in any manner whatsoever without written permission, except in the case of brief quotations in critical articles and reviews. For permissions, contact Influence Publishers http://www.influencepublishers.com.

ISBN: 978-1-645421-36-8 (Paperback)
ISBN: 978-1-645421-37-5 (eBook)

Published in accordance with the U.S. Copyright Office Orphan Works and Mass Digitization report of the register of copyrights, June 2015.

Originally published by Monarch Press.
Frederic Tuten; John D. Simons, 1966
2020 Edition published by Influence Publishers.

Interior design by Lapiz Digital Services. Cover Design by Thinkpen Designs.

Printed in the United States of America.

Library of Congress Cataloging-in-Publication Data forthcoming.
Names: Intelligent Education
Title: BRIGHT NOTES: Crime and Punishment
Subject: STU004000 STUDY AIDS / Book Notes

# CONTENTS

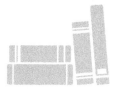

# FYODOR DOSTOEVSKY

## INTRODUCTION

### BIOGRAPHICAL SKETCH OF DOSTOEVSKY

Fyodor Mikhailovich Dostoevsky was born October 30, 1821 in Moscow, the second son of Mikhail, a physician at the Maryinski Hospital for the Poor. The family belonged to the hereditary nobility and possessed a small country estate worked by some one hundred "souls" as serfs were then called. Late every spring the family left Moscow to spend the summer there.

After Fyodor completed his secondary education, his father sent him in 1838 to St. Petersburg where he entered the College of Engineers, a military school run by the Czar. Although he studied hard and in general made a good impression on his teachers, the young cadet was in constant financial straits. Always writing home for more money, he describes his "terrible plight" in the most urgent terms. When money came, though, he celebrated its arrival with a huge banquet and drinking party for his friends, or gambled it away shooting pool. He was generous to the point of self-destruction. When his brother Mikhail was married, Fyodor sent him one hundred fifty rubles. Two weeks later he was broke again, begging him for five. This inability to manage his finances persisted throughout his life. In fact, he was nearly always on the brink of bankruptcy.

Despite his ups and downs in Petersburg, the twenty-three-year-old Dostoevsky became so attached to the city that the mere thought of living elsewhere was unbearable for him. So when he learned that he was about to be posted to the provinces, he resigned his commission and resolved to support himself by writing. In 1846 *Poor Folk* was published and immediately became a best seller. The young author was lionized as the new Gogol, received into the best houses, and became the object of unrestrained praise. The novel is a brilliantly written though sentimental story about the destructive effects of poverty. In quick succession there followed *The Double* (1846) and a collection of short stories under the title *White Nights* (1848).

About this time Dostoevsky became seriously ill, both mentally and physically. Poor, quarrelsome, the victim of unpredictable fevers and convulsions, he soon alienated his admirers as well as his editors. Furthermore, since his erratic behavior was put down to personality rather than to the illness that it was, he was frequently laughed at, jeered, and mocked. Turgenev, for instance, so despised him that he would engage him in conversation merely for the pleasure of torturing him. Still, Dostoevsky was reckoned among the most promising young writers of the day. Unfortunately, his literary career was suddenly interrupted by a remarkable incident that was the direct consequence of his political involvement.

## Sentenced To Death

Ever since the Decembrist revolt in 1825 it had become fashionable for men of learning to promote social reform.

Revolutionary manifestoes were printed abroad, smuggled into the country, and widely distributed. Czar Nicholas I, however, was determined that there would be no revolution in Russia under him. Censorship was severe and many domestic and foreign authors were banned. The penalties for revolutionary activity were increased, and government spies were everywhere. Notwithstanding, Dostoevsky joint a group of political rebels who met every Friday evening at Mikhail Petrashevsky's apartment. Here they discussed different political trends, plotting revolution on the side in a rather harmless way. All the same, the government became suspicious. The members of the circle were arrested, brought to trial, and Dostoevsky, along with several others, was sentenced to death.

Finally, on a cold winter morning after a miserable stay in prison, the future author and his co-conspirators were driven to their place of execution. There, tied to stakes, the unlucky men faced the firing squad. However, as the soldiers were given the order to aim, a horseman suddenly appeared riding full tilt across the square. He bore a letter from the Czar commuting all the death sentences to prison terms. The entire affair was prearranged to frighten them and others of their kind into submission to the Czarist regime.

## "To Live, No Matter How"

Needless to say, Dostoevsky was profoundly affected by this brief encounter with death. So much so in fact that the **theme** of the condemned man appears on countless occasions in his letters, articles, and novels. Among the most forceful passages describing the condemned man's state of mind occurs in *Crime and Punishment* when Raskolnikov says: "Someone condemned to death thinks an hour before his death that if he had to live on a steep pinnacle or on a rock or on a cliff edge so narrow that there was only room to stand, and around him there were abysses, the ocean, and everlasting darkness, eternal solitude, eternal tempests - if he had to remain standing on a few square inches of space for a thousand years or all eternity, it would be better to live than to die. Only to live, to live, to live, no matter how."

Dostoevsky's will to live was severely tested by the Czar's verdict. He was sentenced to four years' hard labor in Siberia followed by another five as a common soldier in a penal battalion. The years of physical hardship, loneliness, and the study of the Bible, the only reading allowed the prisoners, completely changed the author's way of thinking. In both religion and politics he turns into an outspoken conservative, a staunch supporter of the Czarist regime, and the Russian Orthodox Church. He becomes convinced that an Orthodox Christian will, of his own accord, subject himself joyfully to the will of God. Furthermore, by some mystic fiat, a true Russian's political strivings will miraculously coincide with the will of the Czar Emancipator. These attitudes form the basis of Dostoevsky's dialectical thought and ultimately determine whether his heroes are saved or destroyed.

Thus when in 1859, ten years after his arrest, Dostoevsky is permitted to resign from the army and return to Petersburg, we meet a changed writer, but not a less productive one. Shortly after his release he publishes an account of his imprisonment, *Notes from the House of the Dead* (1860). This is followed by the short novel *The Insulted and the Injured* (1861). He even tries his hand at journalism, successfully editing his own paper. Unfortunately, his troubles with the regime are not over. His journal, *Vremya*, is considered subversive and ordered closed. Disgusted, Dostoevsky decides to leave Russia for Europe.

In Wiesbaden he won a large sum of money which allowed him the luxury of an affair with the beautiful, charming, and intelligent Polina Suslova. They toured Europe together visiting all the "in" places until he lost his money. Possessing a destructive passion for gambling, he could not keep away from the casinos. On several occasions he lost everything and had to write friends in Russia for the fare home.

The novel *The Gambler* (1866) is a thinly veiled autobiographical account of this trip. The book is also the third major work in the most productive period of his life which begins in 1864 with the publication of *Notes from Underground*. During the next sixteen years Dostoevsky worked feverishly, producing among other things five major novels and *The Diary of a Writer*. In addition, he maintained a voluminous correspondence with friends, acquaintances, and various admirers who wrote for advice.

## Marriage And Fame

Dostoevsky's existence changed for the better with his marriage to Anna Snitkina, his secretary. Among her many qualities was a good business sense that enabled her to offset her husband's inability to manage his finances. There were trips abroad and every summer the family rented a small cottage in the country. Dostoevsky could now truly enjoy his fame as one of Russia's leading authors and was finally able to write at his leisure.

Yet Dostoevsky's health was always bad. Since his return from Siberia he suffered from epilepsy and these attacks increased with alarming frequency in the 1860s. During the worst period the fits came once a month and so exhausted him that he needed several days to recover. In addition, he contracted tuberculosis in the 1870s which, together with lung cancer, precipitated his death January 28, 1881.

## ST. PETERSBURG: DOSTOEVSKY'S BAD DREAM

The background of many of the author's stories, Dostoevsky's St. Petersburg seems to be a flat, featureless wasteland. Its buildings lack character and its streets are dismal alleyways rarely touched by daylight. To Dostoevsky, St. Petersburg seemed often so unreal that he was haunted by the prospect that it was simply someone's dream and that upon awakening everything would disappear leaving only the marshes and lakes. Others had felt likewise before him. When Peter the Great realized his ambition to build a city upon the Finnish marsh, the peasants living in the vicinity thought that it had been pulled down from the sky. It is only fitting that in such a city human activity is subdued. There is no hustle and bustle in Dostoevsky's city streets, nor do we find the comforting noise of people going about their daily business. Rarely anything takes place in open daylight. The city seems to be condemned to perpetual twilight through which Dostoevsky's characters hurry to their non-descript lodgings.

Thus, Dostoevsky never describes a city in the manner of Balzac. In fact, he had an antipathy toward any kind of description of buildings or landscapes, saying that he had better things to do than waste time over creating word pictures. Consequently, he draws the barest outlines and leaves the reader to fill in the details. From another angle, this method is all the more effective because it allows the reader to create his own image of the city.

We could say that the author conceives St. Petersburg like a map. He chooses a location and then strictly adheres to its dimensions. In *Crime and Punishment*, for example, we know exactly where Raskolnikov lives, how many paces to the moneylender's house, and how far it is to the police station. Often Dostoevsky's favorite places are the ones he personally knows. Central to *Crime and Punishment* is Haymarket Square close to which the author lived for many years. An unbelievably filthy quarter, it is the gathering place of thieves, prostitutes and the like. Surrounding the square are the stalls from which are hawked all manner of merchandise of use only to the destitute. Leading off the square are trash-filled alleyways bordered by pothouses and bodakings of the worst kind. Like Raskolnikov, Dostoevsky loved to wander aimlessly about the place filling his lungs with the fetid air as if he were inhaling the essence of being. Still, precise descriptions of the place are absent. The scenery resembles a rather hastily erected stage set. Yet, we sense it as real because the characters are real, often uncomfortably so.

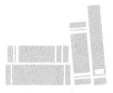

# CRIME AND PUNISHMENT

This novel was written in 1865 and serialized the next year in *The Russian Messenger*. An instant success, the book definitely reestablished its author. The interwoven tale, a veritable odyssey through the human psyche, left many gasping for breath. Robert Louis Stevenson remarked after reading it: "All I can say is, it nearly finished me. It was like having an illness." The book deals with the problems first raised in *Notes from Underground*. Raskolnikov views himself as a wholly superior and independent man free to determine his own destiny according to his own laws. He kills to prove his freedom only to find that he is unable to exist without relating to his fellow men. To escape his loneliness he finally confesses the crime and eventually welcomes the punishment as a first step toward redemption. The conclusion is somewhat forced in that Dostoevsky nudges Raskolnikov into God's camp, saying that freedom is a destructive force if not committed to the principles of Christianity.

## CHARACTERS' NAMES: PRONUNCIATION AND MEANING

The transliteration of Russian names into English is phonetic. Depending on the translation, the author's name is spelled

Dostoevsky, Dostoievsky, Dostoevsky, Dostoyevski, or Dostoievskij. There is no correct English spelling as such. The Russians pronounce it dus-Toy-evsky.

Russian middle names are patronymics, derived from the first name of the person's father. Thus, all the children of the family will bear the same patronymic. The masculine and feminine forms vary slightly.

Raskolnikov, Rodion Romanovich. Rodya for short. (Raskol = split, breaking-off. The Raskolniki is a religious sect that split off from Russian Orthodoxy in the seventeenth century.)

Raskolnikov, Pulcheria Alexandrovna. His mother.

Raskolnikov, Avdotya Romanovna. Dunya for short. His sister.

Razumikhin, Dmitri Prokofich. His best friend. (Razum = reason.)

Alyona Ivanovna. The moneylender.

Lizaveta Ivanovna. Her sister.

Marmeladov, Semyon Zaharovich. Unemployed government clerk. (marmelad = marmelade.)

Marmeladov, Katerina Ivanovna. His wife.

Marmeladov, Sofya Semyonovna. Sonya for short. (Greek sofya = wisdom.)

Svidrigaylov, Arkady Ivanovich. Dunya's former employer.

Luzhin, Pyotr Petrovich. Dunya's suitor.

Lebeziatnikov. Luzhin's roommate. (lebezit = sycophant, fawner.)

Lippewechsel, Amalia Ivanovna. Marmeladov's landlady. (German Lippewechsel = someone who constantly changes his mind.)

Zossimov. Raskolnikov's doctor.

Zametov, Alexander Grigorevich. Police clerk.

Porfiry Petrovich. Examining magistrate.

## A KEY CONCEPT LOST IN TRANSLATION

Prestuplenie is the Russian word for "crime." It comes from pre which means "across" or "trans-" and stuplenie "a stepping." It is similar to the English word "transgression." Thus the Russian concept of crime is a "stepping across" some barrier. Dostoevsky plays upon this concept throughout the novel which, however, is missed in the translation since the English word "crime" has a different etymology.

## THE CENTRAL PROBLEM

Imagine the following hypothetical situation.

Suppose that you have made a scientific discovery of such magnitude that once it is put into practice hunger and disease together with all the scourges of the human condition would disappear from the face of the earth. Everywhere peace and happiness would prevail. But in order to make your discovery known, it is somehow necessary that you kill a hundred innocent people. Does one have the right, or even the duty, to eliminate these people in the name of human progress? The arithmetic is tantalizing. A hundred lives in exchange for universal happiness.

In many ways, this is the central problem of *Crime and Punishment*. The action of the novel revolves around what happens to a young man who kills in accordance with the principle that a wrongful act is permissible if done for the right reasons.

What makes *Crime and Punishment* a great but difficult novel is that the author constantly forces the reader not only to reappraise his conclusions about its central character, Raskolnikov, but also provokes him into carefully scrutinizing his own values. The technique is simple. First, the author enlists our sympathy for the hero by showing him as intelligent and gifted but unable to continue at the university because of poverty. His mother goes hungry for him and his sister is about to sell herself into voluntary concubinage by marrying a rich blackguard. A few blocks away lives a cunning old pawnbroker woman amassing a fortune so as to erect some monument to her soul after death. Based on these considerations, it seems justifiable to kill her for humanitarian reasons. The life of a worthless old hag for many useful ones. Thus, the attacks on our sympathy is quickly transformed into an assault on our values, our judgment. Murder suddenly appears as virtue, evil as good. This reversal of values is in turn reinforced by Raskolnikov's "superman theory." Laws, he declares, are made for the benefit of the ignorant multitude, not for the highly gifted, exceptional people of superior spirit who know what crimes benefit humanity. This theory makes the same kind of claim on our moral system as the first motive, challenging us to reconsider our views.

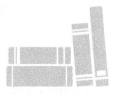

# CRIME AND PUNISHMENT

........................................................................

## CHAPTER ONE

**Theme** And Characterization. Rodion Raskolnikov is a young intellectual in his early twenties. Crushed by poverty, he has been forced to drop out of the university and now lives in a shabby little garret unable to pay the rent or buy food. With no prospects for the future, finding no outlet for his talents, he rages against a society callously indifferent to men like him. When we meet him, he has just about decided to take by force what he needs. His plans are to kill and rob the old woman and use the money to complete his education, launch his career, and perhaps become a general benefactor of mankind. He has spent the past several weeks brooding in his room, planning the crime, and rationalizing the rightness of his undertaking to himself. The story begins as he leaves his room to rehearse the murder.

Dostoevsky is careful to paint a particularly disgusting picture of Alyona Ivanovna, the moneylender. She is a wretched being about sixty with little beady eyes and a neck like a chicken's. She is portrayed as thoroughly malignant, incapable of any feeling of compassion. The chief concern of this human parasite is to amass a fortune through usury which she then plans to bequeath to a monastery so that masses may be said for her soul in perpetuity. She lives together with her half-sister Lizaveta, a simple but good-hearted woman, whom she continually abuses.

Dostoevsky describes Alyona Ivanovna in this repulsive way because he does not want the reader to sympathize with the victim as he would surely do were she portrayed as a kindly person. As will be revealed in later chapters, this is an essential element in understanding the author's views on man's ethical nature.

From the outset we realize that the crime has become Raskolnikov's obsession. Every thought and experience is related to the forthcoming event. He sneaks past the landlady's kitchen because he fears meeting her, then immediately marvels at how he can be terrified of an unpleasant scene with her while contemplating murder. On the street he falls into deep thought, talks to himself, and is completely oblivious to what goes on around him. When a drunk makes fun of his hat, the student suddenly realizes that he must get another one because it is too noticeable and might be remembered.

For the dress rehearsal Raskolnikov has brought his father's silver watch to pawn. His actions in the apartment, his obvious nervousness, and his confusion after leaving the scene of the future murder indicate that he is not yet sure he will carry out the plan. Even on the day of the crime it appears to be chance that forces the action.

After setting the stage for the crime, the author breaks off the narrative to introduce the Marmeladovs, a family with whom Raskolnikov's life will become increasingly interwoven. Raskolnikov does not return to kill the old woman until Chapter Seven.

## CHAPTER TWO

The Marmeladovs. Raskolnikov enters one of the numerous pothouses located in the Haymarket to slake a burning thirst. The place is very dirty, the tables and floors sticky from spilled beer, flyspecks cover the walls, and the stench is nauseating. Yet there is a basic humanity about the place that calms the student's inner turmoil. He feels comfortable here and looks about him in a friendly way. Soon he is drawn into conversation by one of the customers, Semyon Zaharovich Marmeladov, who proceeds to tell him the story of his life.

This little **episode** is by no means a mere exercise in storytelling. Besides relating the circumstances of the family that will have a direct bearing on the novel's outcome, Dostoevsky demonstrates his insight into human nature, and most importantly, introduces his basic belief that men need pain and anguish as surely as food and sleep to feel truly alive. With the possible exception of Razumikhin and Porfiry, not only do the main characters suffer intensely, they often seek it out. For Marmeladov and his wife, however, suffering is self-destructive.

Dostoevsky tells us that a year and a half ago Semyon Zaharovich met Katerina Ivanovna, a widow with three children, formerly an officer's daughter, educated after a fashion. Owing to the death of both her father and husband she was left destitute. So when Marmeladov offered to marry her, she had no choice but to accept. But instead of the gratitude that he expected, she constantly abused him, never letting him forget that she was an officer's daughter and had danced at the governor's ball. She is particularly incensed that she was forced to marry a simple government clerk much below her station and live in a dirty little tenement in the worst part of the capital. Finally, a desperate Marmeladov turns to drink, losing his job as a consequence. Realizing that he could never give his wife the ease of her past life, he unconsciously begins to pursue its opposite. Daily, he drinks himself into a stupor ignoring that the neighbors beat his wife and that the children go hungry. When there is no more money, Sonia, his daughter by a previous marriage, becomes a prostitute in order to provide food for the children. His final act of degradation occurs when he takes the money earned by her for another drunken orgy. Marmeladov is a pathetically ridiculous creature, but we never laugh at him. We feel pity because we understand that he has undergone every experience of degradation in a futile attempt to preserve his dignity as a human being.

Not unlike Marmeladov, Katerina Ivanovna remains an object of pity throughout the narrative. Yet despite the appearances, we realize that she is largely the cause and not the victim of her own misery. By constantly comparing her present husband to her late beloved one and her present living standard to that of her childhood, she drives Marmeladov, who wants to be accepted for what he is and appreciated for what he can provide, into profound desperation. Yet she blames everybody but herself. When she contracts tuberculosis, she uses it as another accusation. She intentionally exacerbates the disease by refusing to close the door to the next apartment although clouds of tobacco smoke pour in. She will not open the windows despite the fact that a terrible stench arises from the staircase. She enjoys irritating her lungs and feels a perverse satisfaction in coughing up blood. From this it is clear that she, like her husband, intentionally exaggerates her destitution. Surprising as it may seem, both have chosen their misery.

---

## CHAPTER THREE

**Theme**. This chapter introduces the theme of Raskolnikov's feelings of inadequacy. As more and more is revealed about the student, we realize that one of the major reasons for the crime is his conviction that he is a useless person and that the murder will be an effort to prove the contrary. The theme of inadequacy is brought out for the first time in the letter from Raskolnikov's mother. This letter provides essential information about the past and introduces several new characters who will play their parts in the rest of the novel. Most important, the letter severely irritates Raskolnikov's already overwrought mind and impels him toward the murder.

The Letter. What at first appears to be a newsy letter from a doting mother is on closer scrutiny a medley of accusations against her son mixed with veiled cries for help for herself and for Raskolnikov's sister. Furthermore, it contains a devastating moral condemnation of her prospective son-in-law Luzhin. The first she accomplishes by the well-worn tactic of introducing each attack with a statement of how much she admires her son and how praiseworthy he is. In this way she is able to convey her displeasure at her son's actions while remaining the devoted mother. For example, she begins by reminding him that he is their only hope for the future: "...you are all we have to look to... You are our all, our one hope, our one stay." She then accuses him of his failures: "What a grief it was to me when I heard that you had given up the university some months ago, for want of means to keep yourself and that you had lost your lessons and your other work." This, of course, under the guise of blaming her own inability to send him money. There follows a list of sacrifices which she and Dunya have made in his behalf, ranging from his sister's humiliating position as governess in Svidrigaylov's house to borrowing money on her own small pension. Finally, she tells her son that his sister Dunya plans to marry Pyotr Petrovich Luzhin chiefly to help Raskolnikov continue his studies. Although she describes Dunya's fiance as acceptable, "It is true that he is forty-five years old, but he is of fairly prepossessing appearance, and might still be thought attractive by women ... though he is not a man of great education, he is clever and seems to be good natured." The reader immediately senses the real Luzhin behind the kind words. He is an opinionated philistine of the worst kind who literally plans to enslave Dunya. Already before meeting Raskolnikov's sister he had decided that for him the ideal wife would be a girl without a dowry yet with an education and of a good family. By marrying her, he would be raising her to his station of wealth and prestige and so be assured of her everlasting gratitude. In short, he looks for a wife who will submit her will permanently to his, regarding him as her benefactor for life.

She reports yet another example of Luzhin's underhanded nature by telling Raskolnikov that when Dunya brought up the subject of assisting her brother in Petersburg, he became evasive and non-committal. Neither did he offer to help with their debts nor will he pay for their trip to the capital. He even lets it be known that there will be no place in his house for his wife's mother.

The meaning underlying the letter is clear. Raskolnikov's mother and sister are at the end of their resources and can no longer support themselves or him. The deprivations suffered for his sake are now to be followed by a culminating act of self-sacrifice in which Dunya will sell herself. It is clear whom the mother holds responsible for Dunya's sacrifice: "Nor has either Dunya or I breathed a word to him of the great hopes we have of his helping to pay for your university studies." The letter ends with the worst news of all for Raskolnikov, the arrival of his mother and sister. He must now confront his unintentional victims, two women whom he loves and whom at the same time he intensely hates for their sacrifices. He is weighed down by feelings of guilt and responsibility. To complicate matters, he is powerless to help.

## CHAPTER FOUR

**Theme.** The letter throws Raskolnikov into a severe depression accompanied by fits of self-contempt. The letter is particularly significant because it marks the end of his lethargical inactivity. He can no longer lie about dreaming of riches and building air castles. He knows he must prevent the marriage at all costs. Furthermore, he can no longer bear the prospect of being further indebted to his family. The necessity to bring some kind of order into his life forces him back to his original plan to kill the old woman. But this time there is a difference. Until this point, Raskolnikov is not fully convinced he will actually go through with it. Now, sheer necessity forces the decision upon him. Viewing the murder form this new perspective, it takes on all the hues of reality. As the magnitude of his plan dawns on him he has to sit down in the street to keep from fainting.

Girl In The Street. A few steps ahead he sees a young girl acting strangely. She appears to move unsteadily, waving her arms about in a strange way. Looking closer, he sees that her clothes are torn in several places and that they are all awry. When she reaches a nearby bench sinking back in exhaustion,

Raskolnikov realizes that she is severely intoxicated. She appears to have been seduced with the help of liquor, or even raped, and then turned out on the street. To the dismay of Raskolnikov, her condition attracts yet another man. He decides to save her by giving a policeman money to take care of her.

Raskolnikov feels compelled to help the girl for several reasons. As we have already pointed out, the young man feels that he is of no use to anyone, and is a burden to his family. By helping the girl he tries to "prove" to himself that he is of use. But his effort is doomed to failure. In the first place he knows enough about himself to realize that he is indifferent to the young girl as an individual and that his act of charity is really an attempt to soften the accusations of his mother's letter. In other words, he is using the girl to buy off his conscience and thus to recover some of his self-esteem. He also realizes that he cannot really change the course of the girl's life. This is clearly brought out when he curses himself for giving the policeman money and speculates that after this experience the girl will probably be turned out by her parents and end as a prostitute.

## CHAPTER FIVE

The Mare Beating. This cruel dream is highly charged with psychological symbols. Dostoevsky was far ahead of his time in using dreams as evidence of psychic illness. The interpretation of the dream is one of the more hotly debated **episodes** of the book. Some authorities suggest that we should take the dream at face value: a little boy watching an incredible display of man's bestiality. Many say that Raskolnikov is the mare while others insist that he is the peasant Mikolka. Each view has its valid points. More likely, Raskolnikov can be identified with all the characters of the dream, the innocent child, the suffering horse, as well as Mikolka and the jeering crowd. The horse is beaten and killed because it cannot pull the load just as the student is being symbolically jeered and derided because he cannot pull the weight of his family. Like the mare, all he can do is kick impotently. Significantly, he awakes with aching muscles and burning eyes, as if he had undergone the beating himself. We may also regard the horse as a symbol of the novel's victimized and persecuted individuals such as the girl in the street, his sister, Sonia, his mother. Marmeladov, even the old money-lender. All of them. For Raskolnikov, the world has revealed its true nature: the helpless are victimized by the strong.

This dream fills the young man with horror because he identifies with the drunken peasant and looks upon the dream as a sign that he will kill the old woman.

Coincidence At The Haymarket. Although, under the influence of the dream, Raskolnikov thinks that he will never go through with the crime, he has an experience that changes his mind. On the way home he passes through the Haymarket and overhears a conversation between two rag mongers and Lizaveta. He learns that the next evening at seven o'clock Alyona Ivanovna will be alone. Taking this event as a sign of providence, Raskolnikov returns to his room delirious, feeling that his will has been seized by an irresistible force and that everything has been decided. As we will see, he commits the murder in just this way. He goes through the motions of the crime almost like a robot obediently carrying out the directives of some master. The "master" in this case is Raskolnikov's idea, his theory of the rights of superior men.

Fate. The narrator tells us that Raskolnikov would not have overheard the fateful conversation if he had not walked through the Haymarket. In fact, to walk through the square involves taking a circuitous route. This is emphasized four times within the space of one paragraph. Here the author introduces the **theme** of Fate which allows Raskolnikov to blame the murder and its consequences on forces other than himself.

## CHAPTER SIX

Background. This chapter and the next are divided into three distinct parts: the psychological and philosophical background leading to the crime is given in Chapter Six. Raskolnikov's preparations immediately preceding the deed and the events of the murder are told in Chapter Seven. The hero had learned about the moneylender the previous winter through an acquaintance. A few months later, he had taken an object to pawn. When he met the old woman he was overwhelmed with revulsion for her. By coincidence, that very evening he learned more about her, overhearing a conversation between a young officer and a student. The woman's personal circumstances and the goal of her greed had affected the two young men in much the same way as Raskolnikov was affected. They expressed the same ideas that were then taking shape in Raskolnikov's mind. Would it not be a great service to mankind to murder the old woman and put the money to good use? Why, it would not be a crime at all because the perpetrator would simply be removing a force of evil. Innumerable lives could be improved at the price of one.

Literary Techniques. That the reader should be informed only now of this essential information is in keeping with Dostoevsky's technique. The author reveals only enough information to focus the reader's attention on the student's reasons for committing the crime. In the Notebooks to the novel, Dostoevsky says flatly that an author must keep his audience in ignorance about the hero's motivations.

We should also point out that for whatever reasons Raskolnikov commits the crime, this is not the central problem of the novel. The author's chief interest is rather with the effect of the crime and the problem of guilt and redemption. Hence, the murder takes place at the beginning of the novel rather than at the end.

Theory Of The Superman. Although we are introduced to the superman theory much later in the book when Porfiry brings out the student's essay "On Crime," it is useful to learn about it here since it represents one of the motives for the murder.

Raskolnikov's essay expands on the idea of the humanitarian criminal. In the article he divides humanity into two classes, the superior and the inferior. Accordingly, he maintains that if the discoveries of Kepler and Newton could not have been made public without sacrificing a hundred or more men, they would have had the right, even the duty to eliminate the men for the sake of making their discoveries known and benefiting the whole of humanity. The laws of society and nature do not exist for the superior men. In different ways, they seek to destroy something in the present for the sake of a better future. Consequently, Raskolnikov reasons that "...if such a one is forced for the sake of his idea to step over a corpse or wade through blood, he can, I maintain, find within himself, in his conscience, a sanction for wading through blood."

The second class is composed of the common herd, men who only serve to reproduce their kind. They willingly live under control. Raskolnikov even believes it is their duty to be controlled because it is their vocation. The first class moves the world and leads it to new goals, the second merely preserves the world as it is and populates it with followers. After Raskolnikov develops this theory, he wonders what Napoleon might have done in his place if he had had no Toulon or Egypt with which to begin his career. What if there had been nothing but the murder of an old pawnbroker as the only possibility to start his career?

Thus, the hero romantically reasons that he should commit the murder to find out whether he is a Napoleon or a member of the common herd. Here it must be emphasized that Raskolnikov is not willing to accept and act on this theory alone. Surprisingly, he casts about for other justifications that are more socially acceptable. He is destitute and needs the money for his education. His mother is hopelessly in debt and his sister is about to marry a blackguard for his sake. With the stolen money he will become a great benefactor and redeem his crime a thousand times over by innumerable good acts.

Thus it is easy for him to justify the crime on humanitarian grounds. An atheist, Raskolnikov is convinced that Christian humility and sacrifice are self-destructive. What kind of a religion asks its believers to accept their fate as "God's will" and do nothing to extricate themselves? Can it be possible that human beings have no right to life? Is it truly moral and Christian that Raskolnikov and his family should be destroyed for lack of money while others like Luzhin and the old woman are allowed to amass fortunes through misdeeds? He is particularly incensed at the idea that Alyona Ivanovna's fortune will be spent on perpetual masses for her soul. Will not her grotesque edifice be erected upon the sufferings of thousands? And, he asks, what kind of God would accept such blasphemous adulation? For Raskolnikov, Christian truth and social justice have become lies.

In motivating Raskolnikov's crime, Dostoevsky has done three things. First, he justifies the crime from economic necessity and in so doing transforms the necessity into a right. Crime is now presented as virtue, evil as good. Next, the author shows that from the historical perspective certain "superior" men are above the law. Finally, he justifies the crime on humanitarian, very nearly Christian, grounds.

After struggling with these powerful arguments, which on more than one level are distressingly believable, we nervously sit back and watch a brutal and savage murder.

While on the surface Raskolnikov appears resolute and determined to carry out his plans for good, solid reasons, on another, deeper level, he realizes the invalidity of his theory. An examination of his actions before and during the crime indicates that he wants to be proved wrong, caught, and punished. He actually works at getting caught. With this in mind let us take a close look at the murder.

## CHAPTER SEVEN

The Murder. On the day of the murder Raskolnikov lies in bed daydreaming about oases, palms, and clear blue waters until it is after six o'clock and really too late to get ready. It soon becomes clear that most of his preparations are faulty. To be sure, he has made a sling for the axe, prepared the false pledge to distract Alyona, and laid out needle and thread. But he has been amazingly careless about the axe. He plans to slip into the landlady's kitchen for it as he leaves, incredibly assuming that no one will be there, then returning it in the same manner. Neither does he concentrate on the final details as he walks through the street. Instead, he fantasizes about fountains and municipal improvements. And, of course, he has forgotten to get rid of his easily identifiable hat. He swears at himself for this oversight, but he does not take it off.

Despite his efforts to sabotage his own plans, luck is with him at every step. He finds an axe in the porter's shed and no one notices him in the street. His entrance into Alyona's house is concealed by a passing cart, and he arrives at the fourth floor landing unseen. He hesitates several minutes on the landing listening to the sounds hoping, so it seems, for someone to come along. Once he is inside the apartment, the old woman conveniently turns away giving him time to get out the axe and strike her with it.

At this point he makes one mistake after another. He snatches up the key ring and runs into the next room. Although he sees that a key will not fit, he tries it anyway. Then he goes back to see if Alyona is dead. While he is filling his pockets with trinkets from the strong box, Lizaveta, the old woman's gentle sister, comes in and he is forced to kill her too. Incredibly, he had forgotten to lock the door. Instead of leaving the place immediately, he wastes several minutes washing the axe and looking for bloodstains. The door is still open! Finally, as if in answer to his desire to get caught, he hears footsteps on the stairs. There upon follows one of the most gripping scenes in literature. The visitors ring the bell and batter at the door while the murderer watches the latch bob up and down in the catch, too petrified to hold it down with his finger. But Raskolnikov's luck holds until the last. While the visitors go downstairs for help, he is able to get out and conceal himself in a vacant apartment on the second floor until he can safely leave.

Viewing the crime in this light, it can be seen that the murderer's actions are hardly those of a man committing the perfect crime. Rather, his behavior indicates that he is bungling on purpose, that he is making every effort to sabotage his crime. The reason, to be more fully elaborated upon later, is simply this: The student unconsciously knows that all his rationalizations are false, that the end, whether for humanitarian or personal reasons, does not justify the means.

# CRIME AND PUNISHMENT

## TEXTUAL ANALYSIS

## PART TWO

........................................................

### CHAPTER ONE

**Theme** And Characterization. Raskolnikov's actions immediately after the murder are an enactment of certain ideas expressed in his article "On Crime." There he wrote that the perpetration of a crime is always accompanied by a disease something like a fever which increases as the crime nears, reaches its peak during the act, and continues unabated for several days thereafter. It is for this reason that most crimes are so easily solved. At the moment of overstepping, the criminal suffers a breakdown of his rational faculties. His willpower is replaced by the most astonishing carelessness just at the time when he is most in need of caution and reason. In other terms, the criminal becomes his own worst enemy because his unconscious mind will attempt to betray him at every turn.

Raskolnikov's essay contains yet another important insight. Most criminals, he claims, not only have a secret desire to be captured but have an even greater one to redeem themselves through suffering. If the criminal happens to be one of those "ordinary" men who do not have the right to overstep, they will punish themselves even more severely than the law: "...they castigate themselves, for they are conscientious; some perform this service for one another and others chastise themselves with their own hands...They will impose various public acts of penitence upon themselves with a beautiful and edifying effect; in fact you've nothing to be uneasy about...It's like a law of nature." These ideas account for Raskolnikov's peculiar behavior after the crime.

Returning home, the student collapses on the sofa, his mind overwrought and delirious. Several times during the night he jumps up in terror, looks for bloodstains on his clothes, paces up and down the room fearing for his reason. He is particularly incensed at himself for making so many mistakes while trying to erase the traces of the crime. Although he remembers to tear out the noose and cut it up, he leaves some blood-soaked rags lying in the middle of the floor. When he undresses and examines every thread for stains, he fails to see that the stolen trinkets make a conspicuous bulge where he has concealed them behind the wall paper. Raskolnikov the intellectual is unable to control Raskolnikov the human being. The following day, and for that matter for the rest of the book, the two sides of his nature are locked in combat. His human side feels guilt and urges him to confess while his rational side struggles to keep him free.

At The Police Station. Raskolnikov experiences a new dimension in terror when he receives a summons from the police. He immediately thinks that the law is on to him and that the summons is merely a ruse to get him out of the room so that it may be searched. So great is the misery of his guilt and his desire to be caught that he leaves the trinkets where they are.

The **episode** at the police station is a study in criminal psychology. Raskolnikov enters with a faint heart and trembling legs, but as soon as he discovers that the summons is concerned with some money he owes the landlady and that he is not under suspicion for the murder, he commences to attract the attention he unconsciously wishes. He gets into a shouting match with Ilya Petrovich, asks questions, and tells the superintendent about the landlady's daughter to whom he was engaged. When this proves ineffective, he faints just at the moment the discussion turns upon the murder. But Nikodim Fomitch is too good-natured to suspect the student and Ilya Petrovich is concerned only with preserving his dignity and so the criminal leaves.

## CHAPTER TWO

**Theme** And Characterization. This chapter describes Raskolnikov's actions just before he is overcome by fever. Believing it is just a matter of time before a warrant is issued for his arrest, he makes haste to get rid of the money and trinkets. His actions, however, are anything but coherent. First he decides to fling the money into the canal, but then he wanders about for hours before finally hiding the stolen goods under a stone. The alert reader will have noticed by now that the student does not look at the trinkets, nor does she count the money in the purse. This strange fact is the first indication that he has not committed the murder for the money. If money had been the primary motivating factor he would, at the very least, have counted it.

His visit to Razumikhin further underscores his spiritual deterioration. He does not know why he has come to his friend's house other than that he intended to do so after the murder. We understand quite well, however, that it is a muffled cry for help.

He asks for work, receives some translating to do along with some money, mumbles something about how much he admires Razumikhin, walks out the door, then comes back ten minutes later to give it back.

The lash Raskolnikov receives from the coachman's whip satisfies in a way his desire for punishment. This is especially apparent if we consider that he purposely walks in the middle of the street, an action that is sure to bring about an injury. Significantly, he accepts the blow as justified. Later, when he flings the coin that a compassionate woman gave him into the water, he symbolically severs the last thread that binds him to his fellow human beings.

That night the agony of his guilt manifests itself in the dream in which Ilya Petrovich mercilessly beats the landlady. The dream signifies his resentment toward his former benefactress for betraying him, his fear of the lieutenant, and his own thirst for punishment. Most importantly, it shows how far his mind has deteriorated in that he can no longer distinguish dream from reality. He is convinced that the beating actually took place.

## CHAPTER THREE

Characterization. Razumikhin traces Raskolnikov to his lodgings intending to repay the insult, but when he finds him unconscious in the grips of fever, he takes care of him. Like Raskolnikov, Razumikhin is a student who has been forced to withdraw from the university for lack of money. But he has not given up hope. He supports himself by giving lessons and doing translations until he can go back to school. Uncomplicated, frank, and outgoing he is extraordinarily cheerful and friendly. He has many friends and everyone likes him. Even Raskolnikov reflects that it is hardly possible to be on any but friendly terms with him. Unlike his friend, Razumikhin knows what he wants, who he is, and what he stands for.

Raskolnikov, however, is not so pleased with Razumikhin. His premeditated rudeness and bad manners severely tax our good feelings toward him. Genuinely liking his sick friend, Razumikhin nurses him, fetches a doctor, and straightens out his difficulties with the police and the landlady. Raskolnikov, however, resents this display of affection and concern which, to be sure, owes partly to the effects of his illness and partly to his general state of mind.

Raskolnikov's actions throughout the chapter indicate that he is not in full possession of his faculties, even though he believes himself to be in full control of the situation. He waits impatiently for the visitors to leave his room and then, instead of doing something coherent, leaps up, races about, empties a beer and falls asleep. He remembers nothing upon awakening.

## CHAPTER FOUR

**Theme.** As in a drama, this chapter serves as an **exposition** in which information is introduced that is essential for future developments. The chapter is given over to a conversation between Doctor Zossimov and Razumikhin who narrates and analyzes the events of the murder as they are presently known to the police. Raskolnikov naturally hears everything although he pretends to understand nothing. He learns that while the police have no real clues to the murderer's identity, they have arrested the painter Nikolay. This simpleton from the provinces, terrified of the police, will later confess to the crime at the precise moment Raskolnikov is about to break down in Porfiry's office.

## CHAPTER FIVE

**Theme** And Characterization. At this point the conversation is interrupted by the entrance of Luzhin, Dunya's fiance. His physical appearance is what one might suppose it to be after reading the letter from Raskolnikov's mother. Plump, stiff, and pompous, he pauses at the door expecting to impress the company with his magnificence. Although he has been in Petersburg only a few days, he has used the time to get himself decked out in new clothes and coiffed in the latest fashion. He looks somewhat imposing but one senses immediately something repulsive about him.

After Razumikhin's and Zossimov's indifference to his appearance deflates his ego, he tries to win their approval by trotting out a few progressive phrases that he has picked up in the last few days such as: "Literature is taking a mature form, many injurious prejudices have been rooted up and turned to ridicule ... In a word we have cut ourselves off irrevocably from the past." However, neither well-turned phrases nor fashionable clothes can hide his baseness for long. Soon we learn that in order to keep his bride in her place he has arranged for them to stay in a squalid apartment near the Haymarket. Luzhin represents everything that Dostoevsky hated in real life: hypocritical respectability, a petty sense of self-importance, and above all the cautious, calculating attitude of the petty Russian middle-class. Small wonder that Raskolnikov is revolted by this creature and insults him in the most savage way.

**Language As Characterization Technique.** Dostoevsky characterizes persons through external appearance as well as through speech. Luzhin phrases everything in stylistic office jargon, speaking as if he were dictating a business letter.

Marmeladov expresses himself in the language of a minor civil servant. He even uses Church Slavisms when describing his suffering and destitution. Razumikhin employs a kind of ecstatic ornamentality while Raskolnikov speaks in short, clipped, hurried sentences.

## CHAPTER SIX

**Theme** Of Alienation. Half delirious, feverish, and weak, Raskolnikov is overcome by a desire to get out into the street and mingle with the crowd. The flight from his room is a symbolical effort to escape from the after-effects of the crime. He wanders aimlessly about, listens to music for a moment, and here and there tries to talk to people who, however, are either afraid of him or take him for a madman. Again symbolically, he is unable to communicate with anyone because the murder has cut him off from society. Even his efforts to converse with a prostitute are futile. We are not surprised to learn that he has about decided to turn himself in to the police.

Crystal Palace. Raskolnikov is sitting in the Crystal Palace Cafe (Dostoevsky uses the Crystal Palace as a symbol for everything he believes is wrong with rationalism and science) reading newspaper accounts of the crime, when the head clerk Zametov notices him and comes over to say a few words. There follows a chilling scene in which the murderer once more tries to incriminate himself. Steering the conversation to crime, the student drops hints that he knows more about the murder than one supposes. He insists that he would never be guilty of such blunders as were committed by the Moscow counterfeiters, a group of criminals currently in the news. Finally, when Zametov asks how Raskolnikov might have killed moneylender, he tells the clerk in detail exactly how he did commit the crime, including a description of the stone where he hid the money. During the course of the conversation he makes five direct **allusions** to his involvement. Though shocked at this peculiar behavior, Zametov thinks the young man is making a joke. Finally, as if absolutely determined to implicate himself, Raskolnikov says: "And what if it was I who murdered the old woman and Lizaveta?" This statement only succeeds in convincing Zametov of the contrary.

Characterization. Raskolnikov seems to derive a perverse thrill from implicating himself, feeling the same cold shivers and tightness in his stomach that he felt listening at Alyona's door just before she opened it. Yet another aspect of his personality is revealed when he meets Razumikhin on the way out. Irritated, he decides to wound his friend. Gloating over the vicious phrases, he tells him to leave him alone, says that he is sick of his face, and shouts that he wants neither his friendship nor his benevolence. Throughout the novel he abuses those who love him most because he regards himself as a "loathsome and vile insect" who has no right to love and friendship.

Murder Scene Revisited: The night Raskolnikov returns to the scene of the crime is probably the novel's most famous **episode**. He rings the bell and feels once more the cold shivers, the terror of that night. He rings a second and a third time, remembering the "agonizing, fearful sensation he had felt then." He walks through the rooms which are being repainted, asks questions about the blood, the murder, the apartment, and ends by giving the porter his name and address. Thus Raskolnikov, unable to live with the consequences of his deed, creates more and more evidence for his own arrest. It is ironic that he must do most of the work himself.

## CHAPTER SEVEN

**Theme** And Characterization. Most of this chapter relates the circumstances of Marmeladov's death and Raskolnikov's further involvement with the family. Walking along the street after revisiting the scene of the crime, the student comes upon a large crowd gathered in the street around a body. Lying on the pavement, his face and chest crushed by the wheels of a heavy carriage, is Marmeladov. Raskolnikov recognizes him and feels compelled to take charge of the situation. He identifies the victim and tips the policemen to get him home.

At the Marmeladov's lodgings the reader is overwhelmed by the extent of the family's misery. The description of the widowed Katerina Ivanovna is particularly vivid. She has terminal tuberculosis and is already coughing blood. Living entirely in the glories of her past, she tells the children romanticized stories of her youth. No longer able to cope with the real world, she transforms events and people into fairy tales. Raskolnikov becomes a rich young nobleman with important connections whom her husband has known for years. She even sees her husband as being under the direct protection of the Governor General.

After Marmeladov dies on the sofa, Raskolnikov gives Katerina Ivanovna twenty rubles, all his money. What is the reason for this generosity? This question becomes especially relevant when we consider how badly he needs the money. Moreover, this was money that his mother raised on her pension. Critics disagree about the explanation. Some claim that his act is a momentary aberration that can be attributed to the aftereffects of the fever. Others point out the similarity to the scene in Chapter Four of Part One in which the student comes to the aid of the young girl in the street. In both cases Raskolnikov is making an attempt to "prove" to himself that he is of use and is not a burden. There is yet a third reason for Raskolnikov's largesse. He is indirectly - and unknowingly - purchasing the family's gratitude and friendship, two things that he badly misses in his life. The scene with Polenka on the staircase shows how much Raskolnikov needs affection and admiration. This experience puts the young man into good spirits and he now decides to call on Razumikhin.

Razumikhin's Party. Raskolnikov goes to Razumikhin's housewarming to make amends for his atrocious behavior of the previous hour. Razumikhin is delighted and forgiving as always. Since his friend is too weak to get home by himself, Razumikhin accompanies him and, of course, lets slip that the police are interested in Raskolnikov's suspicious behavior. While the conversation with Zametov took place only a few hours ago, everyone at the party had already heard about it. Raskolnikov is pleased to learn that he has become the object of intense scrutiny. He is not so pleased to hear Razumikhin say that Zossimov has guessed the cause of his illness. A specialist in mental disorders, the doctor has concluded that the delirium is the product of monomania. Moreover, the doctor had noticed and pointed out to Razumikhin's guests (one of which is Porfiry Petrovich) that his patient is indifferent to everything but the murder.

It is noteworthy that Dostoevsky was fond of putting the most incisive minds into unimposing bodies. Zossimov is short and overweight. The examining magistrate Porfiry, an admirable character, is also physically nondescript.

Notebooks To *Crime And Punishment.* Here it will be worthwhile to mention what Dostoevsky did not put in this chapter. In one of the three notebooks to the novel we learn that he intended to include a scene in which Raskolnikov would attend Razumikhin's party and there reveal his true self. One of the prime motivating factors of the crime was to be Raskolnikov's satanic pride. Arrogantly, he tells the guests that he wants nothing less than to seize power over society and rule like a despot. Throughout the notes, the author emphasizes the hero's exorbitant, devil-like pride and absolute contempt for people. In fact, he was to surrender himself to the police from contempt. While in the final version these traits have been toned down, pride and arrogance remain the outstanding features of the hero's personality.

# CRIME AND PUNISHMENT

## PART THREE

..............................................................

### CHAPTER ONE

**Theme**. This chapter contains several important developments. It introduces Raskolnikov's mother and sister and shows how he feels about them. Furthermore, it indicates the awakening of love between Dunya and Razumikhin.

As we have already pointed out, Raskolnikov stands in a love-hate relationship to his family. Since he is powerless to relieve their poverty and has moreover been a burden to them, he intensely resents their presence because they make him feel guilty. He rejects their expressions of love and hurts their feelings. Even though he has not seen them for three years, he sends them away immediately.

Characterization. This chapter is devoted largely to developing the character of Razumikhin and his relationship to Raskolnikov's sister and her mother. This man is an anomaly in Dostoevsky's pantheon of tortured misfits. He is altruistic, generous, and intensely passionate, embodying all those qualities that the author admired in men and women in general. Accordingly, the two women immediately take a liking to this friendly giant and place their trust in him. For his part, Razumikhin is ecstatic. From the minute he sees Dunya, who is among other things startlingly beautiful, he falls helplessly in love with her. Consequently, he performs all those selfless and slightly absurd acts of which only lovers are capable.

Among Dostoevsky's strong points as an author is his ability to portray women as complete human beings. Dunya is beautiful, self-reliant, and strong. Her pride is offset by an expression of kindness and the ability to show true emotion. Pulcheria, on the other hand, is emotional and shy. She is honest and forthright in her dealings with others and has a sharply defined set of principles. More than willing to compromise, there is a point beyond which she cannot go. This somewhat rigid morality will later be the cause of mental instability when she learns of her son's crime.

## CHAPTER TWO

Characterization. This **episode** allows us to view Raskolnikov from the viewpoint of his friends and family. Over breakfast Razumikhin is allowed to indulge his fondness for talking. Giving his impressions of Raskolnikov, he adds new information that explains much. Although Raskolnikov is basically good and kind, he is either unable or unwilling to show it, feeling perhaps that such traits belong to the common man. In his struggle to prove himself a superior individual, he has become melancholy and proud, never missing a chance to speak insolent, cruel, and ungrateful words. He is impatient, indifferent to the interests of others, and extremely callous. He always seems to be preoccupied with his own thoughts and never listens to what is being said to him. This frame of mind belies his normal childhood and his happy family life before coming to Petersburg. Modern psychology subsumes this kind of behavior under the heading psychological fixation, a kind of mental derangement in which the thinking is focused on a single idea.

Luzhin's Letter. Luzhin's letter further illuminates his base character. Again expressing himself in the stilted jargon of the business world, he makes excuses for not meeting his fiance at the train and for his inability to join them for breakfast. We are not taken in. He is reminding them of their total dependence on him. Next, he announces his visit for that evening and orders that under no circumstances should Raskolnikov be allowed to be present because of the "gross and unprecedented affront" which Luzhin had suffered from him. He then tries to undermine the family's unity by writing that Raskolnikov consorts with women of ill repute and that he has personally seen him give money to one, money which his mother had raised on her pension. This, of course, is a gross distortion the object of which is to repay the student for his insults.

## CHAPTER THREE

**Theme** And Characterization: Beneath the small talk of this family gathering the members are communicating on an unconscious level. So subtly has the author constructed this scene that it calls for close scrutiny. Through facial expressions, intonation, or perhaps choice of words, impressions are made. His mother and sister gradually sense intuitively what they want to know, or better, what they are afraid to know because both sense that something is terribly wrong with Raskolnikov.

His behavior is odd. Though this time outwardly warm and communicative, he does not listen to what is being said. He is dreamy and listless. Only once during the visit does he give way to his thoughts when he marvels at the paradox that people are unhappy if they reach a line they will not overstep and will be unhappier still if they do. This, of course, is a veiled reference to his own predicament.

**Theme** Of Alienation: The author firmly believed that the chief consequence of crime lies not so much in the remorse and despair that overtakes the repenting criminal but in the transgressor's alienation from other human beings. The very act of "stepping over" the boundaries of Christian morality also means "stepping outside" the human community. This is the worst of all possible punishments because man simply cannot endure such isolation. These ideas are illustrated in the present chapter. The young man makes every effort to communicate, asks questions, responds to remarks, tries to tell them about himself. All in vain. His mind always returns to the crime. He, too, is aware of the magnitude of his alienation when he says: "And everything happening here seems somehow far away...I seem to be looking at you from a thousand miles away."

Dunya's Self-Sacrifice. From preceding chapters we know that Dunya plans to marry Luzhin mainly out of dedication to her brother. But she is unwilling to admit the true motive even to herself and so looks for other, more acceptable reasons. She tells her brother that she prefers Luzhin to poverty. Moreover, she has convinced herself that although she does not love her fiance, she respects him and believes that he feels the same way about her. So far-reaching is her delusion that she closes her eyes to all contrary evidence. She explains away Luzhin's parsimony and glosses over his conceit and vanity. Both Razumikhin and Raskolnikov see through Luzhin, but only Raskolnikov knows the real reason for Dunya's actions. She, like her mother, finds satisfaction in self-sacrifice.

## CHAPTER FOUR

Characterization. Thinking Raskolnikov alone, Sonia comes to thank him for his gift whereupon he introduces her to his mother and sister. This is unusual because in Russia at that time prostitutes were considered little more than human vermin not fit to be introduced into polite society. At the risk of belaboring the obvious, it must be pointed out that this is not just Raskolnikov's way of flouting social tradition. He is attracted to Sonia above all as the representative of suffering humanity. Although this **theme** is more elaborately developed in later chapters, it will be well to speak of it here.

It is difficult for the modern student to appreciate the division of classes that prevailed in Russia until the revolution and the role this played in determining a person's life. It was almost a caste system. If, for example, a person was born into the working class, he was condemned to remain in that class for the rest of his life regardless of any special talents he possessed. We are not speaking of the highly gifted who find their way out, but of that vast number of individuals of above average intelligence who find the direction of their lives determined at the moment of birth. Like Raskolnikov, Sonia is such a person. Intelligent, sensitive, and attractive, her life would have been entirely different had she been from the upper classes. Yet all that she can hope for is a life of drudgery, with too many children and an alcoholic husband. Society does not permit her even this lowly existence. Forced into prostitution to save her family from starvation, she lives in misery, loathing herself. Raskolnikov sees in her the eternal victim.

In this scene the reader notices Sonia's beneficial influence on the student. No longer irritable and preoccupied, he engages her in conversation and becomes surprisingly loquacious. The reaction of his mother and sister is noteworthy. While his mother cannot resist expressing her disapproval, Dunya comprehends the situation and goes out of her way to be polite.

## CHAPTER FIVE

At Porfiry's. Raskolnikov has known for some time that he cannot avoid a semi-official meeting with Porfiry, the detective assigned to the case, because the police have two items he pawned, and would arouse suspicion if he did not claim them. Furthermore, the criminal is impatient to find out how much Porfiry knows and if he suspects him. Consequently, he makes careful plans for the meeting.

His first step is to enter Porfiry's apartment laughing, reasoning that a criminal burdened with guilt and terrified of incriminating himself would act differently. So just before arriving he makes fun of the way Razumikhin has washed and combed his hair especially for Dunya. Naturally, his friend becomes flustered and makes a spectacle of himself. Raskolnikov is pleased that they can meet the detective in this casual, unsuspicious way.

There now follows one of the great detective scenes in literature. Dostoevsky's art will be more highly appreciated if we pause to consider that those of us brought up on traditional mystery stories expect something quite different from a detective pursuing his suspect. Modern novels along with television drama have taught us to look for accusations, evidence, denials, alibis, and clear motives. And too, we expect the criminal to be either an obvious villain or a sophisticated, evil genius who dresses expensively and plays Bach on the organ just prior to ruthlessly liquidating a thousand innocent people. Instead of this we are confronted with a chilling battle of wits between two highly unlikely protagonists. Porfiry is round and a little womanish while Raskolnikov is the possessed idealist. Each has the reader's sympathy and we find ourselves in the ridiculous position of hoping that both will win.

Porfiry has also made careful plans for the encounter. Knowing that he has no evidence to connect Raskolnikov to the crime, he nevertheless suspects his involvement and opts for the psychological approach. For his part, the student facilitates Porfiry's task because even here he cannot **refrain** from incriminating himself. Using innuendo, allusions, an occasional wink of the eye, Porfiry throws Raskolnikov off balance. The detective also notices that when the suspect feels himself on strong ground, he becomes insolent and defiant while when the questions get too near the truth, he becomes pale and his lips tremble. These and other almost imperceptible hints begin to convince Porfiry that Raskolnikov is the murderer. At last, the detective employs the well-known police tactic of putting the criminal at ease only to spring a trap when the suspect is off guard. At the end of the chapter Porfiry asks him if he happened to see two painters working in the second-story apartment the evening he visited the moneylender. We know, of course, that the painters were there on the night of the murder, not when the student went to pawn his father's watch. But Raskolnikov sees through the trap in the nick of time.

Nature Of Crime. While Porfiry spins his web, the conversation turns to the causes of crime. This is one of Dostoevsky's favorite subjects. Speaking through Razumikhin, he deflates the fashionable nineteenth-century contention that crime is a protest against the iniquities of the social order, that murder, rape, and mayhem can be ascribed to social imperfections. In other words, crime will cease if society is made more equitable. The proponents of this view devised all manner of mathematical formulas for the perfect society. Dostoevsky believed that such utopianistic thinking does not take human nature into account and therefore is doomed to failure from the beginning. He maintained that this kind of philosophy leads to an ultimate stage of moral deterioration where freedom and the worth of the individual are no longer respected. Dostoevsky, however, does not deny the possibility that man may eventually discover the formula for a perfect social organization. Sometimes he seems convinced that such a faultless system already exists, hidden somewhere in the hearts and minds of people, and that one day we will find it.

Economic Utilitarianism. It will be recalled from the previous discussion of Raskolnikov's theory that he has divided humanity into two unequal groups, the ordinary and the extraordinary. The ordinary man has to live under control, has no right to break the law simply because he is inferior. It is his duty to obey the law. But the extraordinary man has the right and even the duty to transgress the law if it is essential for the realization of his idea. In other terms, Raskolnikov's theory claims the existence of principles that transcend the law and that sanction crime - even bloodshed - if the act results in the ultimate benefit of humanity.

Raskolnikov has chosen a utilitarian morality in which the end justifies the means. Dostoevsky strongly opposes this kind of utilitarianism because it reduces human life to a matter of economics. Ultimately, such a view cannot lead to universal harmony but to mutual annihilation. To him, this theory is more frightening than any official authorization to take life because not only does it negate the Judeo-Christian morality which is the basis of Western civilization, it sets another anti-Christian code of ethics in its place. The extraordinary man is not just a person who disobeys the law, he is his own law.

## CHAPTER SIX

Man In The Overcoat. If the novel's most famous scene occurs when Raskolnikov returns to the pawnbroker's apartment to ring the bell, the **episode** at the beginning of this chapter ranks a close second. Coming out into the courtyard of his house, the porter shows Raskolnikov a man in a long overcoat who has been inquiring about him. But when the student approaches, the man turns and walks away. Apprehensive, the criminal overtakes him and asks for an explanation. Without stopping, the man looks him straight in the eye and says "murderer." Though numb with fear and scarcely able to breathe, Raskolnikov walks at his side for another hundred paces and asks in a barely audible voice what he means. With a smile of hatred he replies: "You are a murderer" and disappears into the crowd.

**Theme**. This experience leads to a scene of brutal self-analysis. Back in his room the student reveals for the first time how he really feels about the crime. To begin with, he admits that he is unable to take the consequences of his action: "And how dared I, knowing myself, knowing how I should be, take up an axe and shed blood! I ought to have known beforehand...Ah, but I did know." He murdered for a principle, wanting to prove not only that he had the freedom to do so but also the right. He suffers greatly because his theory proved unworkable: "The old woman was only an illness...I was in a hurry to overstep...I didn't kill a human being, but a principle! I killed the principle, but

I didn't overstep, I stopped on this side...I was only capable of killing. And it seems I wasn't even capable of that."

This is the crux of the novel. Unable to kill with impunity, Raskolnikov despairs. Why then, is he unable to bear the weight of his crime? To understand this question fully, we must consider Dostoevsky's views on rationalism, the nature of freedom, law, and ethics.

Freedom And The Law. Many thinkers of the eighteenth and nineteenth centuries held that man, with the proper kind of education, could become an entirely rational creature. These rationalists believed strongly that we eventually would be able to solve all our problems through the reasoning process. Others went even further, claiming the existence of laws governing human behavior much like those governing the physical universe. Both the rationalistic and the deterministic explanation of man were anathema to Dostoevsky. There was yet another current of thought upon which we have touched here and there that incensed the author: the contention that man is totally free. Some of Dostoevsky's contemporaries (whose spokesman is the Underground Man) refused to accept an a priori good or evil in their world. For them, human actions are devoid of value until their value is determined at the moment of choice. Today we call such a theory situation ethics, knowing fully that in such a world of relative values conventionally good deeds may be bad and vice versa. Such views disturbed Dostoevsky who saw that if there are no inviolable laws - and there can be none if one is to be totally free - each of us is his own law, a situation in which humanity could not survive.

Dostoevsky's Ethics. Dostoevsky's ethics are rooted in Christianity. His conviction that Christianity is the foundation of man's ethical behavior derives from his speculations about the historical development of culture and religion. It must be emphasized that the Russian author had a very special conception of Christianity and how it affects our daily lives.

Dostoevsky saw clearly that for Western man Christianity is not just a religion, it is a way of life that pervades every aspect of civilization. He realized that when that religion first established itself as the dominant force in Europe, each person from childhood to maturity was under increasing pressure to conduct himself according to Christian teachings. Soon religion and the prevalent culture became one. Religious ethics penetrated customs, laws, the whole social framework. Each succeeding generation internalized the heritage and reinforced its terms to the point where even the atheist is forced to play his part in this on-going process.

Thus for Dostoevsky culture is within us. Culture and the personality are a unit, indivisible, and mutually dependent. Each decision, every moral choice, each value judgment, everything we do and think is in accordance with the total personality. A person can no more exclude cultural heritage from his personality than he can exclude the unconscious.

Dostoevsky's conception of the interrelationship between culture, religion, and the personality implies a truth about man as an ethical creature. Each man is a reflection of his heritage and he carries within himself a system of absolute values and a clear conception of the Good created in the image of Christianity. Dostoevsky believes that moral absolutes are functional inner laws that guide Western man. If this quasi instinctual knowledge of right and wrong is transgressed, psychic disintegration will result. As we have pointed out before, Dostoevsky is not a rationalist. For him, it is not reason that impels us toward the

Good but the heart, the spirit. If a person refuses to listen to his heart, ethics become a matter of convenience. Morality loses its foundation, freedom becomes amoralism. Dissolution awaits the man who infringes those inner absolutes.

The Crime Reexamined. In the light of the foregoing let us take another look at the crime. Raskolnikov begins with a simple question: Are there any moral limits in human nature or is everything permissible? Concluding that there is no God and thus no sacred canons, he comes to the tempting delusion that everything is allowable and proceeds to an act of crime. His encounter with total freedom, however, ends in a spiritual disaster. He murders with the intention to confirm his theory only to discover soon thereafter that man's ethical nature forbids the killing of even the most harmful person. With the old woman he kills all hope to find a guiding principle for his life outside the traditional moral framework. At this point, however, he does not comprehend what is happening to him. His confusion is reflected in the dream in which he tries to kill Alyona a second time.

Raskolnikov's Dream. The dream is composed of elements from recent experience. The man who beckons is the same one in the overcoat who called him a murderer. The student follows him through the streets to Alyona's house, goes up the staircase, and finds himself once again in the moneylender's apartment. Everything is the same as on the night of the murder. The events that follow are a symbolical reenactment of the crime. This time the deed is presented not as it actually happened but as it affected him. Seeing an object in the corner covered with a large cloth, he thinks it is the man in the overcoat. But when he looks, he sees Alyona bent double, hiding her face in her lap. Removing the axe from the noose, he strikes her with it. When nothing happens, he bends down to look but she too bends lower. He gets down on the floor and looks at her face from below and is horrified to see that she is silently shaking with mirth, doing her best to conceal it. Overcome with frenzy, Raskolnikov strikes her again and again, but the harder he hits the louder she laughs. Rushing onto the staircase he sees that all the doors are open with people silently staring at him. Paralyzed with fear, he can neither scream nor move.

The dream dramatizes the hero's predicament and passes judgment on his existence. In the beginning Raskolnikov had hoped that the crime would give purpose and direction to his life and perhaps define his potentialities. Now we understand why Alyona laughs at the failure of his efforts. The young man has attempted to put himself above humanity and has failed. Striking the old woman is merely a symbolical flailing out against the impersonal forces that are closing in on him from all sides. As the dream reveals, all struggle is ineffectual and hope is a delusion. The magnitude of his powerlessness dawning at last, Raskolnikov stands on the staircase immobilized by terror, vainly trying to scream. It is the noiseless scream of impotence.

This scene is one of Dostoevsky's most poignant comments on the human condition. He is saying that life without God, without the living sense of the Good as the guiding principle, is indeed devoid of meaning.

# CRIME AND PUNISHMENT

.....................................................................

### CHAPTER ONE

**Theme** And Characterization. Considering the unsavory reputation that has preceded Svidrigaylov, our first impression of him is good. His frank, unpretentious nature leads the reader to seriously question the judgment of his detractors. He appears in an even more favorable light when compared to the pretentious Pyotr Luzhin. Svidrigaylov is open and genuine, commanding both respect and interest. Nor can we resist admiring a person who appears to have accepted himself for what he is and who lives at peace with himself. Like the reader, Raskolnikov is impressed and cannot believe that this is the man about whom such gruesome stories are told. So incongruous is the man and his reputation that Raskolnikov accuses him of not being Svidrigaylov at all but an imposter. Furthermore, this man from the provinces has the honor of being the only person in the novel who deeply interests the hero.

Yet despite his many qualities, Svidrigaylov is a dark figure. He is neither a good person nor an evil one. Right and wrong are abstractions to him with little real meaning. He is a moral drifter. He lives from day to day following his inclinations without direction. Furthermore, whether he rapes a young girl or indulges in some charitable action, he remains emotionally aloof. Eternally adaptable, he is equally at home at Prince Svirbey's and in the Haymarket. At first glance he seems to have found the freedom for which Raskolnikov searches so passionately. His colorful past includes cardsharping, robbery, even murder. All seemingly without lasting consequences on his conscience. Yet we soon learn that he has paid a terrible price for his transgressions. Freedom from ordinary limitations has brought abject boredom. His ennui is not psychological but **metaphysical** in nature. Recognizing no spiritual force outside himself, he holds nothing sacred, believes in nothing, wants nothing.

This boredom is apparent in almost everything he says. He is not offended by Raskolnikov's rudeness simply because it does not matter. He listlessly passes from one subject to another clearly uninterested but hoping to hear something new from the student. He tells us that because of boredom he went with his wife to the country and then remained there simply because he was not interested in going anywhere else. Even the ghosts that appear to him are boring. The shade of his wife chats about trifles and is not even angry when he tells her of his plans to remarry. Svidrigaylov's view of eternity accurately reflects the emptiness of his life: "We always imagine eternity as something beyond our conception, something vast, vast. But why must it be vast? Instead of all that, what if it's one little room, like a bathhouse in the country, black and grimy with spiders in every corner, and that's all eternity is?" Such a conception of eternity is in accordance with his overall philosophy of hopelessness.

Eternity to him is merely a spiritual continuation of earthly existence. In this figure Dostoevsky exposes the bankruptcy of the philosophy that declares all things permissible. Freedom from responsibility means eternal boredom. When Svidrigaylov fails in his project to win Dunya, from whom it seems he expects some sort of salvation, the eternal ennui becomes unbearable and he shoots himself.

Svidrigaylov is in Petersburg for the sole purpose of convincing Dunya to elope with him. In his usual way, he stops at nothing to get what he wants. To find her, he tells her brother that he only wants to see her once more to apologize for the way he treated her and to make her a present of ten thousand rubles. To prove his intentions are honorable - a clever maneuver - he tells Raskolnikov of his plans to remarry.

It is worth noting that Raskolnikov's indignant refusal of the money casts further light on his motive for murdering the moneylender. If he really had killed for the money as he says, then why does he refuse ten thousand rubles with no strings attached? Because he did not murder for the money but, as he later says, "for himself alone."

## CHAPTER TWO

**Theme** And Characterization. Dunya has insisted on her brother's presence at this family gathering to bring about a reconciliation between him and her fiance in order to avoid having to choose between them. The effort is futile. Luzhin is offended that Dunya would even consider putting her brother on the same level with him, her benefactor, and refuses to discuss it. He becomes overbearing and insulting in the certainty that his power over the two women is so great that he can behave with impunity in any manner he chooses. As we recall, he keeps them helpless and without money on purpose, so as to gloat over their dependence on him. Now he is completely taken aback by Dunya's rebellious attitude. When Raskolnikov unmasks the lie and malicious intent of Luzhin's letter, he becomes enraged, completely losing control of himself. It is ironic that the businessman's final and almost unbelievably distorted insult of Dunya should also reveal his own mean and spiteful nature. Dunya displays black ingratitude, he says, in ignoring the fact that he has condescended to take her as his wife despite her questionable reputation in regard to Svidrigaylov. In return for this magnanimous and selfless act, he might be justified in expecting some display of thanks. Now at last, he cries: "I see myself that I may have acted very, very recklessly in disregarding the universal verdict." The scene ends when Raskolnikov, pale and trembling with anger, orders him to leave.

## CHAPTER THREE

**Theme** And Characterization. Fifteen minutes after Luzhin's departure, the family is in the best of spirits discussing plans for the future. Suddenly, Raskolnikov prepares to leave, frightening everyone with his strangeness. Again Dostoevsky dramatizes the crime's effect on the perpetrator. His deed has alienated him from life to such an extent that he is unable to enjoy the warmth of an intimate family gathering. It has destroyed his capacity for happiness along with his ability to express or feel affection. There is nothing more for him to do other than to leave.

A strange scene takes place between Raskolnikov and Razumikhin who has followed him into the corridor. They stand in silence beneath the lamp, Razumikhin straining every nerve to comprehend his friend's state of mind. Then some unspoken message or hint passes between them and Razumikhin perceives the truth. Although horror-stricken, he does not pass judgment, feeling instead sympathy and understanding.

## CHAPTER FOUR

**Theme** And Characterization. Although Raskolnikov visits Sonia to confess his crime, he is momentarily deterred by a fascinating puzzle. How is it that Sonia has been able to live in misery without going mad? How can she continue to hope when Katarina Ivanovna coughs blood and will likely die in a week. Can it be that Sonia does not realize that she will have to provide for the children, a task for which she is not equipped? With no money and a precarious profession, Raskolnikov knows quite well that she and the children will come to a dismal end in the Haymarket. Yet Sonia has hope. The student is further mystified by the fact that as a prostitute Sonia lives in depravity, yet it does not touch her, it has not penetrated her heart or changed her personality. Circumstances to the contrary, she remains innocent and virtuous. What is the source of her strength? The answer proves to be simple. She has implicit faith in God.

Sonia is Dostoevsky's portrait of suffering humanity, the archetypal victim. She is not only unequal to the struggle of life, it terrifies her. Meek and self-effacing, she has no capacity to resist the forces that are closing in upon her. She even experiences displeasure in resistance and so passively endures the evil and suffering that circumstances bring. As Sonia is presented, her only hope, and by extension mankind's, is faith in God for it enables her to cope. When Raskolnikov challenges her faith she answers simply: "What should I be without God?" This kind of faith is incomprehensible to Raskolnikov because to believe in God is to act according to God's will which in turn means to relinquish free will, something that he is yet unwilling to do. Small wonder that after Sonia reads from the Bible, he concludes that she must be a "religious maniac."

Lazarus. Raskolnikov asks her to read from the Bible. At first she hesitates because it involves revealing the secret treasure that has sustained her through the years of misery. The Bible is like a retreat for her and to read it to Raskolnikov is letting him know about her innermost secret. Yet she has a tormenting desire to share because she senses Raskolnikov's despair and need for help. In selecting the story of Lazarus she offers him a way out of his soul sickness. There is a parallel between Lazarus' physical death and Raskolnikov's spiritual one. Just as the Biblical figure is raised from the dead so can Raskolnikov gain hope and new life through Christianity. This is brought out in the way Sonia reads. She trembles with emotion and quivers with fever the nearer she gets to the miracle. She reads the words triumphantly, her voice clear and powerful, convinced that no one could hear and not believe. But Raskolnikov does not see the parallel. Envious of her enthusiasm, he begins to torture her, reducing her to tears in a matter of minutes. Not only is she a prostitute, he says, Polenka will also become one and her little brother will be begging on the street corner before he is seven. What is more, Sonia's sacrifice is in vain for she has debased herself for nothing. There is no hope for the likes of her or him, neither in Heaven nor on earth.

Nevertheless, Raskolnikov is deeply affected by the immensity of Sonia's suffering. It more than matches his own in intensity. It is for this reason that he wants to confess the murder to her. Desiring neither forgiveness nor sympathy, the important factor is the act of confession itself. And it is highly important to whom such a confession is made. It must be someone who knows.

It is impossible to say with certainty when Raskolnikov begins to love Sonia, but it likely dates from the moment he identifies her as a companion in suffering. Here one cannot speak of love in the sense of passion or desire but rather of empathy or agape. He feels drawn to her because he identifies her "crime" with his own. In a sense she has transgressed as grievously as he, for in submitting to prostitution she has not only injured herself but she has cut herself off from humanity as well. Despite what Raskolnikov says, there is a difference between their crimes. Unlike Raskolnikov, Sonia retains her self-respect and hope for a better life. It should be noted in passing that Dostoevsky carefully subdues any outward expression of their love.

Sonia As Double. In many respects Sonia can be regarded as Raskolnikov's double. Both live alone separated from society by their acts. Both need faith in an idea that can redeem them in order to survive. Their lives touch at the point where Raskolnikov's faith in himself is completely shaken. Yet as ever, he needs to believe in something to give direction to his life. Later in the novel, Porfiry accurately points out that Raskolnikov is one of those men who would smile under torture as long as they believe in what they are doing. In a way, one aspect of Raskolnikov's character, the impulse to living faith, is already fully developed in Sonia. Eventually he will permit her to become his teacher.

## CHAPTER FIVE

Psychology Of The Criminal. In preparing this scene Dostoevsky consulted manuals on criminology, interviewed detectives, and when the draft was completed, sought authoritative opinions. The result is a complicated battle of wits between a criminal who knows the psychology of a detective and a detective who is no less familiar with the behavior of a criminal. Raskolnikov, for instance, knows that it is a tradition among detectives to stalk their prey from a distance, to begin the interrogation with a harmless subject to distract the suspect and then, at the precise psychological moment, deliver a fatal, knock-down blow with a surprising question. In fact, he accuses Porfiry of using this tactic. What course of action remains to the detective when his subject knows all the tricks? How can someone be disarmed who knows what is going on? It is a tribute to Porfiry's genius that the answer is as simple as it is effective.

Porfiry begins by giving an impromptu lecture on the psychology of the criminal. He fabricates a hypothetical culprit to illustrate his theories but the reader soon notices that the hypothetical case bears unmistakable resemblances to Raskolnikov. It is part of Porfiry's plan never to categorically state whether he suspects the student for in this way he keeps him in a state of constant anxiety. He knows that suspense is a very useful tool in a criminal investigation, especially when evidence is lacking.

Modern psychology has confirmed Porfiry's views. Man appears to prefer a direct accusation or even imprisonment to the terror that accompanies a sustained period of suspense and uncertainty. Paradoxically, as Raskolnikov's behavior indicates, the more intelligent the person, the more unable he is to endure uncertainty. He will either go insane or unconsciously try to incriminate himself just to put an end to the torture. As we know, Raskolnikov vacillates between the two. When not delirious he tries to confess either directly to someone or indirectly by  returning to the scene of the crime.

Thus, in this **episode**, Porfiry proves himself a master of the criminal mind. Not only is he practical but he is also knowledgeable in the ways of human behavior. On the one hand, experience has taught him that if an investigator locks up his subject too soon, he may deprive himself of further important information. On the other hand, he understands that physical escape is meaningless for Raskolnikov since he searches for peace of mind. Consequently, Porfiry observes Raskolnikov almost with an air of amusement as he lies, trying to cover his tracks in the most clever fashion. The detective is sure that the student will eventually behave more and more out of the ordinary before finally giving himself up. We already know of such behavior. He faints in the police station, annoys the police officers, and makes a general nuisance of himself. Porfiry is so sure of his tactics that he explains them to the student. Furthermore, he levels with Raskolnikov, telling him that he knows about the evening he returned to the scene of the crime.

Raskolnikov's Reaction. Raskolnikov hates Porfiry because he is a symbol of the law and represents the rewards of a law-abiding existence. Raskolnikov wants to look upon the law as an inconvenient obstacle from which he, the liberated man, is free. But as he has discovered, he is not free of the law, he has not been able to transgress it with impunity. He not only hates himself for his weakness, he also hates Porfiry for being right. And too, he detests the detective for demonstrating with his own life that happiness and satisfaction can be found within the law. Finally, he despises Porfiry for giving him what he unconsciously needs, the continual uncertainty that will eventually force him to admit the fallacy of his theory and confess. At this point the interview is interrupted by an unexpected event that completely alters the course of the interview.

## CHAPTER SIX

Nikolay's Confession. Nikolay the painter bursts into the room and confesses that it was he who killed the old woman and her sister with an axe and robbed them. Of course, Porfiry does not believe him, but since the interruption has ruined his plans, he has no choice but to release Raskolnikov.

As it turns out, Porfiry planned to deliver his knockdown blow after all. Behind one of the doors sits the man in the overcoat who called Raskolnikov a murderer. At the precise moment of Nikolay's interruption, Porfiry was about to confront the suspect with his accuser. This man had arrived in Porfiry's office a few minutes before Raskolnikov. The information he gives the detective convinces him beyond any reasonable doubt that Raskolnikov is the murderer. It further accounts for the disconcerted way he acts toward the student and why he does not believe Nikolay's confession. This new information acts as a catalyst, allowing Porfiry to see everything from a different perspective. All parts of the riddle now fall into place. Raskolnikov's fainting at the police station, his illness after the crime, his exaggerated laughter when he arrives at Porfiry's rooms, his eerie conversation with Zametov, all point to his involvement. Most importantly, the clue shows Porfiry how to handle his suspect. Since Raskolnikov's actions indicate that he wants to get caught, all Porfiry has to do is let him know that he is suspected and the culprit's own temperament will do the rest. It makes little, if any, difference in the detective's calculations that Raskolnikov could learn of these tactics later.

# CRIME AND PUNISHMENT

## PART FIVE

### CHAPTER ONE

**Theme**. This and the following two chapters are a tour de force of characterization held together by the story of Luzhin's incredibly underhanded attempt to revenge himself on Raskolnikov by having Sonia arrested for theft.

Characterization. Luzhin's attitude to his dismissal by Dunya is quite predictable from what we know of his character. He does not see that it is his own fault but blames it on Raskolnikov and admits only to a few tactical errors. Had he, for instance, been less parsimonious and spent a few hundred rubles on a trousseau, some jewelry, and presents his position would have been stronger. Anyway, he reasons with regret, there would not have been any risk since Dunya and her mother are people of character who would have felt obliged to return any presents given them. He believes his error consists in not having obliged the two women enough to himself. It never occurs to his calculating mind that his own character brought about the rupture.

In whatever Luzhin does there is a petty motive. Instead of finding his own place when he arrives in Petersburg, he moves in with his former ward Lebeziatnikov. Although miserliness is the chief purpose, he also thinks to profit in other ways. Having heard in the provinces about certain circles consisting, he imagines, of powerful revolutionaries, he wants to get on their good side through the intervention of Lebeziatnikov who belongs to these groups. Not because he finds their ideas attractive but because he is afraid of them.

Lebeziatnikov. It is well known that Dostoevsky had little patience with the so-called nihilists, iconoclasts and such of the 1860s and 70s. He was particularly in censed at the Westerners, a group which slavishly imitated everything European. He thought that their ideas, imported wholesale from Europe, had little to do with the problems peculiar to Russia or the Russians. Consequently, he never lost an opportunity to caricature them mercilessly.

Lebeziatnikov is Dostoevsky's portrait of a sycophant of an idea. Dull and superficial, he attaches himself to whatever idea is in fashion and thereby vulgarizes it. For example, many genuine thinkers of the last century pointed out that the concept of "possessiveness" is the cause of much human anguish. The very idea that people look upon a person, such as a wife or a husband, as "property" deprives that person of his/her worth as an individual. They urged the rejection of this value in favor of a more generous, non-possessive attitude. Incapable of understanding the true nature of this idea, Lebeziatnikov trivializes it by proclaiming that he would urge his future wife to take a lover so that he might demonstrate how progressive he is. The basic superficiality of such thinking is revealed in his wish that his parents were alive so that he might have someone to shock by his liberality. His mind is constantly occupied with such trivial but "progressive" problems as "Should a member of the commune be required to knock before entering the room of a fellow member?" or "How many free marriages are too many?" Finally, the shallowness, even hypocrisy, of his liberalism is revealed in his treatment of Sonia. As a liberal he has no theoretical objections to prostitutes, but when he learns that Sonia has become one, he complains to the landlady, saying that he is unable to live in the same house with her.

Luzhin's Plan. Luzhin has developed a complicated plan to avenge himself on Raskolnikov by hurting the person he knows the student cares for. He calls Sonia to the apartment on the pretext of contributing ten rubles to her needy family. But while he is talking, he surreptitiously slips a one hundred ruble note into her pocket. Later, Luzhin will appear at the funeral dinner and accuse her of stealing it from the table, demand that she be searched, and when the money is found, have her arrested. The plan would have succeeded had not Lebeziatnikov accidentally seen him put the money in her pocket. It is a most fitting **denouement** that Luzhin should be subjected to the one experience he dreads most, humiliation.

## CHAPTER TWO

**Theme** And Characterization. What at first appears to be a funny story about a funeral dinner gone awry is on closer examination a profound study in psychology. As we know from previous chapters, Katerina Ivanovna is a fairly well-bred woman brought up in a genteel household, and educated at finishing school. Within the space of two years her position deteriorated from respectability to abject poverty. She did not just exchange one stratum of society for another by marrying Marmeladov, he fell to the very bottom of it. Poverty itself she probably could have tolerated, for she is a brave woman. What she cannot cope with are the values of her new neighbors, their rudeness, and their general ill manners. Living in a society where the dividing lines between classes have been largely effaced, it is difficult for the modern student to appreciate what this means for Katerina Ivanovna. It does not mean just moving from one economic plateau to another, it means the adaptation of a new and lower set values. Now with the death of her second husband she foresees even more misfortune in store for her. This set of circumstances, coupled with a terminal case of tuberculosis, more than explains the grandiose arrangements for the funeral dinner.

When we observe the festivities, we see that the dinner is not so much given to honor the memory of Marmeladov, but to show the lowbrow lodgers that she still knows how to do things properly when the occasion demands. The meal is of the greatest importance for Katerina Ivanovna and she wants it to proceed with dignity and honor. Yet precisely because of her aristocratic pretensions, the celebration ends in a tragi-comic hullabaloo.

This **episode** is characteristic of Dostoevsky's way of telling a sad story as if it were a comedy. His technique consists in constantly focusing the reader's attention on the ridiculous. First, he shows how Katerina is particularly incensed because the more respectable lodgers have refused the invitation. Instead, there is a motley crowd of ne'er-do-wells who have come to take advantage of the free dinner without bothering to attend the funeral. In a display of the most grotesque manners in the tradition of a Fellini film, the guests gobble, slurp, and belch their way through the meal. Clinging to the last vestiges of more happy times, Katerina Ivanovna babbles about her "almost aristocratic" heritage, and for the one hundredth time, tells how she is an officer's daughter and once danced at the governor's ball. Her pretensions goad the guests into provoking an argument between her and Amalia Ivanovna, the obtuse landlady. Pandemonium is averted only by Luzhin's arrival.

## CHAPTER THREE

Luzhin's Humiliation. Although revenge and hatred for Raskolnikov figure prominently in Lushin's plan to accuse Sonia of theft, he has yet another, more important reason. If he can prove that Sonia is a thief on top of being a prostitute, he can demonstrate to Dunya and her mother that he was right in condemning Raskolnikov for properly introducing her to them. In other words, he is seeking an occasion to prove her a disreputable person. He is hoping, of course, that Dunya will take him back and that Raskolnikov will be permanently alienated from the family. However vile, the plan is well conceived, masterfully executed, and might have succeeded if it had not been for Lebeziatnikov's intervention. The events that now take place read like the script for a vaudevillian melodrama.

The villain solemnly enters the dwelling of a destitute family just returned from burying the head of the household and proceeds to accuse the innocent and unfortunate daughter, appropriately dressed in rags, of larceny. The accusation is made in the most believable form and succeeds in turning almost everyone present against the unhappy girl. Her protestations of innocence are unavailing. She is told that if she does not confess, the matter will be turned over to the police. A search of the girl's pockets turns up the one hundred rubles, neatly folded in eight, placed there previously by the villain. Outraged innocence, heartbreaking cries, and pitiable wailing that would cause the very stones to melt. The landlady orders the Marmeladovs to vacate the apartment immediately. Fortunately Lebeziatnikov comes to the rescue shouting "How vile," and gives a long-winded but revealing explanation that he personally had seen Luzhin place the bank-note in Sonia's pocket and, although it is "against his conviction," is prepared to swear on the Bible. The mother falls at his feet in abject gratitude. The guests do not know whom to believe. The villain is about to regain the advantage. At this crucial juncture Raskolnikov delivers the humiliating coup de grace by explaining how Luzhin was turned out of his family's house the night before and that the entire plot is a cheap effort at revenge. Crushed, the villain leaves the scene in disgrace.

We have described the **episode** in this way to demonstrate how Dostoevsky can take the most trivial material and breathe life into it. He is successful where so many fail because he never loses sight of human nature. It does not require a great deal of imagination to understand Luzhin's hatred, Sonia's terror, Lebeziatnikov's outrage, or even Katerina Ivanovna's despair. While we may not be able to identify with the magnitude of their feelings, we nevertheless experience the same thing on a smaller scale every day.

## CHAPTER FOUR

Confession. Raskolnikov's confession to Sonia finally reveals the true reasons for the crime and how the deed affected him. Standing at Sonia's door wondering why he must tell her, Raskolnikov senses intuitively that he is at a turning point. He feels it. Italicized in the original, this word hints at the fundamental change taking place within the criminal. For the first time he rejects reason in order to act in accordance with the promptings of his heart. Feeling also tells us why he comes to Sonia. He senses that she is close to being the embodiment of Christian love and the very image of innocence described in the Scriptures. She is that rare kind of person who experiences no conflict between the promptings of reason and feeling, she simply knows in her heart what is right and wrong. This is evident several times in the course of the conversation.

When Raskolnikov finally tells Sonia of his crime, he begins by posing a hypothetical question. If, he asks, Sonia were somehow permitted to choose whether Luzhin or Katerina Ivanovna should live, whom would she select? Of course, the question is a trap designed to make his own crime appear in a more favorable light because in preferring the life of her stepmother to that of the abominable Luzhin, she would be playing Raskolnikov's game of value judgment. In choosing, she would be guilty in thought of a crime similar to the one that Raskolnikov had committed in reality. But Sonia refuses to answer the question, not because she perceives the trap but simply because it is contrary to her nature to even conceive such a thought: "...who has made me a judge to decide who is to live and who is not to live?" And so Raskolnikov must confess without her becoming a spiritual accessory to the crime.

It is extremely difficult for him. He cannot even bring himself to utter the words "It was I who killed the old woman and her sister and robbed them" because at this point it is just beyond his strength. Several times he attempts to pronounce the words but his lips refuse to obey. Finally, he asks his friend to guess the identity of the murderer and when she cannot, simply says: "Take a good look."

Sonia's reaction to the confession is indicative of her character. She is not upset by the fact that Raskolnikov killed the old woman and Lizaveta, who was her friend, but by what has happened to him. She sees from the anguish in his face that the true victim of the crime is Raskolnikov and her compassion goes out to him in the astounding words: "...what have you done to yourself?"

The basic goodness of Sonia's character also compels Raskolnikov to admit to himself the true reasons for the murder. This is an excruciating task because it is an act of self-confrontation. He intuitively knows that sooner or later he will have to strip away the false conceptions that he has constructed around himself until the true Raskolnikov will stand naked and alone. He senses that until he faces himself and bears the pain that his final death and rebirth requires, his life will be a living hell. On the other hand, he fears the agony that self-scrutiny will bring.

This fear leads Raskolnikov through a labyrinth of rational excuses before he finally tells the truth. At first he retells the now familiar story that he killed in order to prove to himself that he is spiritually akin to Napoleon and also destined for greatness. He explains again that for a long time he wondered what that man would have done if there had been no Egypt or Toulon with which to begin his career. What if there had been nothing but an old woman who had to be murdered so that he might take her money for his career. Would he have felt guilty about such a petty crime, or would he have committed the act without even thinking about it? Raskolnikov concludes that it would neither have caused him anguish nor would it have struck him that it was not a monumental deed, and that he would have strangled the old hag without hesitation. Thus Raskolnikov says that he killed to find out if he was a "Napoleon" or not. Sonia's only response to this explanation is to insist that he tell her the real reason.

In a second desperate attempt to justify his deed, he claims again that concern for the welfare of his family prompted him to crime. Is it not, he cries, a gross injustice that he should be condemned to a life of drudgery as a petty bureaucrat or a clerk in some office with a paltry salary, unable even to provide for the bare necessities for his mother and sister while some vicious old woman creates a monument to her soul? It is far better that he use the money for a better purpose. But Sonia is not taken in by this whitewash. The very notion that human beings can be evaluated in terms of dollars and cents is alien to her. More importantly, she senses that the student also sees the fundamental error in this theory and so begs him again to tell the truth.

Murder For Curiosity. Finally, Raskolnikov tells the truth. He wanted to see how he would feel after a murder! In his own words: "I wanted to find out then and quickly whether I was a louse like everybody else or a man...whether I have the right." Thus, his family's welfare never really influenced his decision nor was he greatly interested in becoming a leader of mankind in case he discovered that he had the "daring" to step over the laws of society and ignore basic human rights. *The why*

Unlike the murderous deeds of great historical figures, however, Raskolnikov's crime had no other purpose than to satisfy his curiosity about which class of men he belonged to. As we know, he told himself that if he could murder and feel nothing, this would prove to his satisfaction that he was a man of superior spirit. On the other hand, if he suffered the symptoms of the common criminal which he enumerated in his article "On Crime" - fever, guilty conscience, loss of reason - this would mean that he belonged to the inferior group. We learn, though, that Raskolnikov is crushed not only because the crime affected him in this "inferior" way, but also because he begins to see that the whole concept of inferior and superior man is probably a sham.

Although we risk sounding repetitious, it will be easier for the reader to empathize with Raskolnikov if he understands in greater detail his philosophy of life.

Inferior Man. The terms "inferior" and "the common herd" as Raskolnikov uses them describe a state of mind rather than an economic class. The man of common spirit seeks above all else to establish equilibrium between the countless extremes of which human nature is capable such as reason and passion, duty and inclination, nature and spirit. It is precisely between these absolutes that Raskolnikov's common man seeks his place. He keeps the extremes of which human nature is capable at a distance. Anger is permitted, but not rage; love, but not passion; happiness, but not ecstasy. In short, ethical absolutism is anathema and a superficial peace of mind is far preferable to the fire of total commitment. Since Raskolnikov's common man is by nature a weak and fearful creature, content with a lukewarm existence, he is easy to rule. The civilization that he creates for himself reflects his weakness and insecurity. Strength, force, and self-reliance are a burden to him. He gladly abandons responsibility to "higher authority."

Superior Man. By contrast, Raskolnikov's man of superior spirit, whom he dreamed to resemble, regards himself as wholly independent. He rejects all ethical standards not his own and views human life as meaningless unless it serves his goals. He is strong. Neither physical hardship nor loneliness will faze him. He realizes that as long as a man identifies with the group, he cannot develop his potentialities. Thus, the superior man is one who has succeeded in gaining almost absolute freedom not only from society and its value systems but also from the deterministic influences of his own human nature.

Raskolnikov feels a special kinship with the men of superior spirit for he too searches for meaning in a chaotic world. He sees no place for himself in a dehumanizing society whose values are conformity, consumption, and hedonism. The murder is as much a desperate effort to break out of is confining existence as it is to find out if he is superior. The crime may even be an effort to propel himself into that class. To Raskolnikov's way of thinking, his inability to kill with a clear conscience condemns him to the inferior class.

Despite what he thinks, he does not belong to that group. He is a true human being wandering somewhere between the two, sharing elements of both but belonging to neither. He longs to make the final break and join the ranks of what he imagines to be the superior, but he is unable to do so because that involves denying his very human qualities. Thus Raskolnikov's error consists in having established a theory for himself that fails to take into account the complexity of human beings in general and his own in particular. He does not realize that all men are composites of hereditary and cultural influences that determine our lives. Raskolnikov, whether he likes it or not, was raised by parents in accordance with Christian thought. Hence, he has internalized such prohibitions as "Thou shalt not kill" and for him to act against such a taboo means to act against himself. The murder becomes, therefore, a crime against the Self. "I murdered myself, not her." The punishment for the transgression will be - despite all self-righteous justifications - some sort of archetypal guilt feeling.

The Solution. What alternatives remain to all the Raskolnikovs of the world who exist in a state of intense dissatisfaction? How can they create meaning for themselves in an indifferent universe or find a place in a dehumanizing society? If they transgress, how can they redeem themselves? The answer lies with Sonia and her doctrine of love and faith. Even Raskolnikov's disturbed mind realizes that Sonia is the way out of his isolation and soul sickness, the pinpoint of light at the end of the tunnel. What he needs is not more reason and abstractions, but life, feeling, and love, to live in the world and take part in it.

## CHAPTER FIVE

**Theme** And Characterization. This chapter recounts the events of Katerina Ivanovna's madness and death. The insults she receives at the funeral dinner provoke her to rush off for help to Marmeladov's former chief who is entertaining guests. When the attempt to seek justice from higher authority fails and she is unceremoniously thrown out of his house, she embarks upon a course only her deranged mind can conceive, the attempt to earn her living as a street entertainer. Raskolnikov and Sonia find her and the children on the street surrounded by a crowd of jeering spectators. Exhausted, gasping for breath, and rigged out in an absurd costume, she frantically rushes about trying to fit her new role. One minute she is coaxing the children to sing and dance, only to beat them in desperation when they do not understand. Squabbling with the spectators, singing infantile songs, and babbling about her genteel origins, she finally collapses on the pavement. Later, dying in Sonia's room, her delirium is punctuated by such incoherent ejaculations as: "Your excellency...well born... one may say aristocratic." These and other similar phrases lead us to see a parallel between her and Raskolnikov.

Brotherhood Of Fantasy And Theory. We remember that when Katerina Ivanovna's fortunes began to decline, she tried to preserve her sanity by retreating into an elaborate fantasy. The further she sank into degradation, the more fantastic became the daydream. When the reader meets her, she remembers her father, a simple captain, as a colonel who was "almost a governor." Though of the middle class, she has long since convinced herself of her "genteel, one may say aristocratic" background. After Marmeladov's death, she remembers him not as the chronic drunkard he actually was but as a good provider who served his country "in truth and fidelity, and one may say died in the service." Furthermore, she thoroughly believes that her husband's former chief is the cause of their misfortune. But the events of the funeral dinner bring reality crashing down upon her. Her air castles destroyed, she sinks into madness and death.

As Katerina lives through her fantasies of aristocracy, Raskolnikov sustains himself through his theories of the superior man. Like her, he cannot live with the fact that his life does not measure up to his expectations. Like her, he blames others for his misfortune. While Katerina Ivanovna escapes into fantasyland, he compensates for his failure by erecting an elaborate theory that allows identification with the world's greatest men. As Katerina clings to her fantasies, he cultivates his theory like a religion. Yet he can comfort himself with such delusions of superiority only as long as they remain unchallenged. When he tries to act in accordance with this creed, it almost destroys him.

Here we encounter again the basis of Dostoevsky's ideas about the human condition: Without faith, man is nothing. In the following chapters Raskolnikov comes precariously close to Katerina Ivanovna's fate before finding salvation.

Svidrigaylov. Once again Svidrigaylov leads the reader to question the authenticity of his reputation as an evil person. If he is so insensitive, why does he tell Raskolnikov that he will take care of the funeral arrangements, place the orphaned children in a suitable institution, and rescue Sonia from her fate? And again, even though he eavesdropped on the student's confession, he does not take advantage of this information in any way. If the reader wishes to speculate how a truly base person might respond, he has only to imagine Luzhin in possession of Raskolnikov's secret.

# CRIME AND PUNISHMENT

## PART SIX

...............................................................

## CHAPTER ONE

**Theme.** While Raskolnikov is not insane in the ordinary sense of the word, it is clear that he is mentally unbalanced. Lucidity and confusion alternate. When he comes to the defense of the women, he is alert and articulate. As soon as he reflects on his own existence, however, he forgets facts, imagines experiences, and spends whole days in deep depression without food or drink.

In this chapter we find Raskolnikov completely alone for the first time since the crime. He is plagued by an indefinable mood that makes him feel uneasy. He tries to escape this "uneasy presence" by seeking out lonely places and taking solitary walks in the countryside. But the more isolated the place, the more he senses the unseen presence and he hastens back to the city to mingle with crowds in taverns and cafes. The feeling, though, persists and he realizes that he must come to some kind of understanding with his life and the events of the last ten days but finds he cannot. This sense of malaise coupled with a vague, ill-defined fear is Dostoevsky's way of describing an archetypal guilt feeling at work.

Characterization. Razumikhin is at his wits' end because he cannot understand how anyone in his right mind could treat his family like Raskolnikov does. His only explanation is that his friend is mad. In fact, he had heard several rumors to this effect. At any rate, Razumikhin at this point had decided to insult Raskolnikov and then wash his hands of the whole family before going out and getting good and drunk. But when he meets Raskolnikov he happens to be quite reasonable and succeeds in dispelling such thoughts by simply mentioning that he and Dunya had spoken of him, Razumikhin, the day before and that both had agreed on his superior human qualities. When Raskolnikov mentions that Dunya senses Razumikhin's love, the young man leaves enraptured, cursing himself that he suspected his friend of the murder that night under the street lamp. Now he believes that his friend is a political conspirator about to embark upon some desperate undertaking and that Dunya is part of it. His conviction grows firmer the more he thinks about it.

Razumikhin must not be regarded as merely simple-hearted and gullible. Like Sonia, he is a genuine human being reluctant to think bad of his fellow man. It is precisely because of these qualities that he is easily misled. Yet he possesses extraordinary insight. He intuitively senses that Raskolnikov may be guilty of murder, but prefers other explanations for Raskolnikov's behavior as long as possible.

## CHAPTER TWO

Porfiry's Psychology. In this chapter Porfiry has another chance to display his ability to manipulate subjects. Changing his tactics because he is now convinced of the student's guilt, he puts aside his professional tricks and treats the young man with sympathy and respect. He is no longer the detective mercilessly pursuing the criminal as in Chapter Five of Part Four. He now becomes a father figure who tries to help Raskolnikov regain his self-respect through confession. Finally, he lays all his cards on the table, relating how he suspected the student's guilt long before he and Razumikhin came to his house and how Raskolnikov's behavior gradually transformed his suspicions into conviction.

Porfiry tells the student that he will have to arrest him soon. Despite this warning, the detective is not concerned that Raskolnikov will run away. A common criminal would try to escape, but not this man. As mentioned before, both Porfiry and Raskolnikov know that a person cannot run away from himself. Eventually, he would return of his own accord because he needs the suffering to gain redemption. As Porfiry says: "You can't get on without us." Italicized in the original, these words introduce one of the chief **themes** of the novel, the doctrine of salvation through suffering.

Nature Of Suffering. Dostoevsky firmly believed in the regenerative power of suffering, considering it essential for the expiation of guilt. Furthermore, suffering voluntarily accepted leads to spiritual rebirth. The nature of suffering and its role in Dostoevsky's novels will be clearer if we pause to consider its position in Russian thought.

Ranking as one of the chief characteristics of Russian Orthodoxy is mysticism, the belief in the possibility of direct communion with God. This communion does not depend on any outside factors such as revelation, or answers to prayers. Rather the highest communion is achieved by direct imitation, or identification which enables the soul to partake of the divine essence. The mystic accepts symbolism as literally or metaphysically true. In this state of mind, God ceases to be an idea and becomes an experience. Since Christ's greatest moment on earth was his suffering and death for humanity, the Russian feels that when he suffers he approaches Christ in both a mystical and literal sense.

This mystical-religious disposition and the belief in the absolutism of suffering is a result of the peculiar history of Russia. It is one of suffering. Christianity was the people's only comfort during the centuries of immeasurable hardship when it was at the mercy of other nations. These traditions and legends of the people emphasize the conviction that the weak, the insulted and the injured will, at the Last Judgment, be exalted above the domineering aristocracy from whom and for whom they endured such anguish. The dictum "The meek shall inherit the earth" has real meaning for them.

The Russian ideal, then, finds expression in suffering as a spiritual bond between men and God. If we consider for a moment the actions and life of Christ, we can better understand the significance of this bond. The difference between the Old and the New Testament determines man's relationship both to himself and to humanity at large. The Ten Commandments are concerned chiefly with actions, whereas Jesus' law focuses on feeling-the love of God and one's neighbor. If action is subordinated to feeling, the concepts of sin, freedom, and law undergo a basic change. As Christianity developed in the West, however, the importance of actions rather than states of mind continued to be stressed. According to Jesus, laws can be fulfilled only through humility and love. He had infinite patience with thieves, drunkards, and harlots and reserved his wrath for the Scribes and Pharisees whose actions might have been irreproachable but whose feelings and minds were corrupt. Likewise, Dostoevsky portrayed murders, prostitutes, and alcoholics as basically good people whereas he viciously attacks men of empty actions, merchants, bureaucrats, in fact the whole hypocritical middle class. The Russian interpretation of Christianity, therefore, tries to do justice to the primitive status of being. Feeling!

Nikolay's Actions Explained. The religious sanctity of suffering accounts for the actions of Nikolay, the painter. After a few days in prison he voluntarily confesses to the murder, not because he is under pressure to do so but because he is thirsting for punishment. Of course, Porfiry does not believe him and orders an investigation. The inquiries turn up the revealing information that in addition to a very strict religious education, several members of his family belonged to a primitive religious sect which exalted suffering above all else and that Nikolay himself had been the disciple of a certain mystical elder. In the solitude of his cell he thinks about the elder and the Bible which leads him to regret his life of profligacy since coming to Petersburg. So by accepting punishment for a crime of which he is innocent, he will be able to expiate his real, or imaginary, "sins." Similar to Nikolay's are the actions of a prisoner Porfiry once knew who spent his time with the Scriptures, finally reading himself into a frenzy. One day this prisoner succumbed to the desire for punishment, seized a stone, and threw it at the governor, aiming a few feet to one side so as not to injure him. Porfiry says: "Do you know, Rodion Romanovich, the force of the word 'suffering' among these people! It's not a question of suffering for someone's benefit, but simply 'one must suffer.'"

We now understand the significance of Porfiry's words when he tells Raskolnikov that he needs punishment if he is to rejoin the human community. We also understand better why the detective is not afraid that the criminal will run away: "I am convinced that you will decide to take 'your suffering'...For suffering, Rodion Romanovich, is a great thing...Don't laugh at it, there's an idea in suffering, Nikolay is right. No, you won't run away, Rodion Romanovich."

Sonia, too, knows what Raskolnikov must do, but she feels in her heart what Porfiry perceives through psychology. When Raskolnikov asks what he can do to be rid of the agony, she replies that he must go the crossroads, kiss the earth that he has defiled, and finally bow down to all humanity saying aloud that he is a murderer. "Then God will send you life again ... Suffer and expiate your sin by it, that's what you must do."

But Raskolnikov is not yet ready to take his punishment. He must first to go Svidrigaylov and meet the ultimate consequences of his ideas.

## CHAPTERS THREE AND FOUR

**Theme.** This and the following chapter, which we shall treat as one, show Raskolnikov at the crossroads. Not yet ready to confess, he has two alternatives. He can either continue the struggle with Porfiry and risk losing his mind altogether. The terms Dostoevsky uses to describe the student make it clear that this is a real possibility. His hesitation to choose the latter course is understandable because it involves more than confession. It is the agonizing admission that he has been defeated without ever being caught. So he first goes to Svidrigaylov hoping to find another way out of the predicament, to hear something that will fill the void left by the collapse of his theory. Instead, he discovers that this man lives from day to day, which means that the vacuum in his soul is just as profound as Raskolnikov's.

Necessity Of Faith. Svidrigaylov's curse consists in the fact that he has no idea, no principle around which he can organize his life. He dissipates his energy in debauchery and other vices. Yet even as an atheist he recognizes the necessity of believing in something as the first premiss of a meaningful existence. Disillusioned by unsuccessful attempts to find meaning in human action, he is drawn to people who have something to live for. He admires Sonia for her implicit faith and he is drawn to Dunya because she has succeeded in organizing her life around self-sacrifice. Had she lived in the second or third century A.D., he tells her brother, she would have ecstatically endured torture and martyrdom as a Christian, while had she lived in the fourth or fifth century she would have lived in the Egyptian desert for thirty years sustaining herself on locusts and ecstasies.

As we have already pointed out, Svidrigaylov suffers from metaphysical boredom. And it is from boredom that he comes to the capital, hoping that Dunya can provide him with what he needs. When he meets Raskolnikov, he is also drawn to him. It is one of the novel's ironies that these two men seek each other out to learn something new, but when they meet they are like two mirrors set opposite each other reflecting nothingness.

Svidrigaylov And Dunya. A considerable portion of Chapter Four concerns Svidrigaylov's relationship to Dunya. According to his side of the story, she was strongly attracted to him from the beginning. He maintains that her emphasis on chastity prevents her from expressing what she feels in a normal way. Instead, her desire for him manifests itself in a messianic effort to lift him out of his depravity and rededicate him to a useful life. How else, he says, can one account for her continually following him about and even weeping over him? By way of illustration, he tells Raskolnikov about a married woman he once knew who acted in a similar way. Virtuous, faithful, and chaste, she could not admit to herself that she was just as eager as Svidrigaylov to make love. In order to do so she had first to delude herself that the seduction was an accident, a moment of weakness. Svidrigaylov concludes with the observation that Dunya, too, would have succumbed had he not been so impatient during the preliminaries. The reader would be justified in dismissing this analysis of Dunya's feelings as delusions of male chauvinism were it not for the events of:

## CHAPTER FIVE

Svidrigaylov And Dunya (Continued). Svidrigaylov coaxes Dunya into meeting him secretly in his apartment. This gives rise to the question why she agrees to a private meeting with an unscrupulous person she knows to be passionately in love with her and of whom he is afraid. Certainly not in response to his letter which hints at her brother's crime because the first thing she says when entering the room is that she has already heard the rumors and does not believe a word. And again, why did she not ask Razumikhin to escort her? The same questions occur to Svidrigaylov, and he also notices how she quickly changes the subject when he mentions these facts. We also observe how frequently the color rushes to her face, how she is often scarcely able to speak from excitement, and the difficulty she has in keeping to the topic of conversation. These and other minor details, insignificant in themselves but revealing when viewed as a whole, are evidence that she does feel an attraction for him. We feel that she agrees to the rendezvous for one reason: To find out how she feels about him.

Some critics disagree on this point, claiming that Dunya comes solely out of concern for her brother. Furthermore, they insist that Svidrigaylov's object in getting her alone is to rape her, and that he is unable to do so because he is impotent. Judging from what we know of this man's character, however, it is difficult to imagine that he would have been incapable of lovemaking had she been willing. Furthermore, were he truly impotent there would not have been much point in setting up the meeting. It is true that he does not rape her, but only because he loves her so much that he cannot bring himself to treat her like the serf girls at his country estate.

Dunya's moment of cognition comes with a feeling of disgust when Svidrigaylov attempts to touch her. When he finally understands that she neither wants nor loves him, the blow is so crushing that he lets her go.

## CHAPTER SIX

Svidrigaylov's Suicide. Dunya destroys whatever hopes he had for a new life. But even if she went with him, his soul sickness would likely have returned after a short time. He simply has nothing to live for, no goal or object which can absorb his considerable strength. To repeat, in Dostoevsky's view, freedom and genius are of little value if not governed by a guiding principle. Genius dissipates itself in trifles and freedom becomes a force of destruction, turning upon and annihilating itself.

The moment Dunya leaves the room Svidrigaylov decides to commit suicide. He spends the last evening of his life in a small hotel located at the outskirts of the city. His room merits special attention. It looks like an attic, so low and cramped that he can scarcely stand up in it. The wallpaper is torn and yellowish, there is dirt in every corner, and there are flies all around. It was in just such a room that Raskolnikov conceived his theory of humanity and plotted the murder. Ironically, Svidrigaylov spends his last evening in a room remarkably like his conception of eternity, "like a bathouse in the country, black and grimy with spiders in every corner."

That night, Svidrigaylov's past returns to haunt him in the form of two dreams. The first recalls a spring day with sunshine and flowers. It stars Svidrigaylov himself morbidly contemplating the body of a young girl who had killed herself after having been raped. In the second dream, he sees a reflection of his own depravity in the face of a five-year-old girl he had tried to help. He watches with horror how her innocent expression is transformed within the space of a few seconds into the provocative expression of a common harlot, the mirror image of his own lust. These dreams force him to view himself in perspective. Desperate, he leaves the hotel.

No longer able to face himself, he ends his wasted life in the street. At the moment he pulls the trigger, Raskolnikov, who has also been wandering about the city all night, is looking into the rain-swollen waters of the Neva also contemplating suicide. When he turns away from the swirling torrents, he rejects Svidrigaylov and his philosophy of unlimited freedom in favor of Sonia and what she stands for.

## CHAPTER SEVEN

**Theme** And Characterization. The conversation with Dunya just before he goes to the police reveals Raskolnikov's attitude toward the crime. It should be pointed out once again that outwardly he feels no remorse. For him, killing Alyona remains a humane act. Nor does he regret having shed blood. He still insists that men of superior spirit understand that crime is simply a matter of definition, a social convenience. Yet Raskolnikov discovers that despite the rationalizations, his conscience does not give him any peace. In his present state of mind the only possible conclusion for him is that he is a weak coward, "a beggarly, contemptible wretch." At this point, Raskolnikov's decision to confess is motivated more by the desire to punish himself for his weakness than because of any real change of heart.

Walking along the street toward Sonia's house, he watches the multitude running to and fro, knowing that each of them is a criminal at heart, each quite capable of killing a thousand old women. He cannot understand how he can feel any guilt toward them. Neither can he comprehend the system of punishment ordained by this "herd of sheep." He knows that they will send him to prison not for the sake of regenerating him, but for revenge.

## CHAPTER EIGHT

Characterization. During the final moments preceding the confession to the police, Raskolnikov abandons himself to self-hatred. So intense is his disgust with himself that he regards genuine emotion as a further sign of his despicability, and he punishes those toward whom these feelings are directed. While it wrings his heart to say good-bye to his sister, he abuses her instead, and when she turns around to look after him on the street, he angrily waves her away. At Sonia's, to pick up the crucifix, he laughs at the symbolism of "taking up the cross," and when he realizes that she wants to accompany him to the police station, he drives her away like a dog.

Walking along the street, he suddenly realizes that going to Sonia's for the cross was just a ruse to cover his desire to see a friendly face and draw strength from her anguish. Again, he

85

indulges in self-contempt and mocks himself bitterly for having these human and therefore "contemptible" needs.

Kissing The Earth. Among the scenes by which the novel is remembered long after our first impressions have died away is Raskolnikov's bowing down to the earth. In this act he acknowledges the earth as the mother of all humanity, the primary source of being. He also humbles himself before the "herd" he previously despised. Bowing down to the people is a symbolic act which not only marks the beginning of his transformation into a living human being but also his desire to rejoin the human community. The novel ends with the words: "It was I killed the old pawnbroker woman and her sister Lizaveta with an axe and robbed them."

Time. Most readers are surprised to learn that the action of the novel covers only two weeks, that of Part I three days. Actually, there is no real lapse of time in the story because the novel relates an experience. Everything that does not bear directly on Raskolnikov's situation is excluded. Instead of time, there is a rhythmic contracting and expanding of tension.

## Epilogue

The Epilogue recounts the events of Raskolnikov's trial and describes his situation in Siberia after his conviction. Although the student's conduct is exemplary after his arrest and he gets a relatively mild sentence because of it, he is still not convinced that taking a life, any life, is forbidden to man. The confession of the crime has not brought him the peace of mind for which he hoped. He is driven by a "vague and objectless anxiety" and thus keeps reflecting upon his crime without ever really coming to terms with it. Having exhausted all other excuses, he now blames his deed on fate, claiming that at the critical moment he was seized and forced to act by a will greater than his own. Instead of taking responsibility for his actions, he views himself like the hero of classical tragedy who is destroyed in a battle with blind destiny.

Raskolnikov's regeneration begins nine months after his arrival in Siberia at Easter. The symbolism is interesting. The human gestation period is linked to Easter, traditionally associated with rebirth and resurrection. At that moment we find him in the hospital suffering from wounded vanity, outraged pride, and physical exhaustion in that order. He still feels no remorse for what he has done to himself, to his family, and friends. Moreover, the future seems as bleak as ever. Then suddenly he has a revelation in the form of a dream.

He dreams that humanity is attacked by a new form of the plague that deludes its victims into thinking that they had finally found a philosophy of life based on truth governed by the power of intellect. Yet, each individual believed in a different truth. The result, of course, was chaos. Only a few people survived. The dream carries Raskolnikov's theory of the rights of superior men to form their own destiny to the extreme. It is the author's way of telling us again that God's laws are needed to protect mankind from itself.

Although Raskolnikov does not speak of the dream as if he understands its true meaning, his changed behavior thereafter reveals a new man. When he is released from the hospital, he discovers that Sonia is ill and therefore cannot visit him. Now for the first time since their relationship began, he finds that he misses her. Then when she finally comes a few days later, the criminal is all at once overcome by his new-found sense of humanity of which she now becomes the symbol. He falls to the ground before her, throws his arms around her knees and weeps bitterly. Doing so, he embraces what she represents: The striving for identification with Christ through suffering.

Although this transformation happens suddenly, with almost no preparation, it is in accordance with Dostoevsky's doctrine of salvation through suffering. We are told that this scene by the river is only the beginning, the first step of his rebirth and that he must undergo more anguish and suffering before he can rejoin the community of men. Throughout his writings, Dostoevsky emphasizes that only the person who is truly alive suffers. Anyone who does not suffer is outside of life, a prey to dark and primal urges that constantly threaten to plunge him into despair. If the alienated man is to regain Christ, he must first immerse himself in life with its sufferings and afflictions. It is Dostoevsky speaking when he has Marmeladov explain: "Every human being, though he may be struck in dirt up to his neck, is really living only when he suffers and consequently needs Christ, and consequently there will be Christ. Only those do not believe in Christ who are truly not alive and whose soul is similar to an inorganic stone."

*do something like this, at least let us know beforehand!*

To add to the puzzlement, Jesus responded with a question of his own: *Why were you looking all over town for me? Didn't you think that I would be drawn to this place?* Remember this.

Luke tells us that they didn't *this* understand what Jesus meant at that moment. But Mary wanted to understand more fully, so she stored this incident in her heart and pulled it out from time to time to reflect on it. She didn't just stew over the way Jesus had treated her and Joseph; she asked what it meant. What was

prayerful pondering helps us gain a bigger picture—one that has room for God's love and provision.

So don't be afraid to ask tough questions, just as Mary did. Just make sure you also return to the central truths that Mary clung to: God loves me and he has a plan for my life, even if I don't fully understand it now.

*"Immaculate Heart of Mary, draw me into loving conversation with your son."*

▲ **2 Corinthians 5:14-21**
**Psalm 103:1-4, 9-12**

For spiritual reading this week, see the article on page 10.

Jesus will welcome us into his heavenly kingdom?

First, we can remember that Jesus himself will be our judge. On the cross, he promised the criminal beside him, "Today you will be with me in Paradise" (Luke 23:43). He refused to condemn the woman caught in adultery (John 8:10-11). He welcomed tax collectors into his kingdom, including Matthew, who became one of the Twelve and a saint (Matthew 9:9-13). These Gospel stories give us reason to believe that he will treat us with mercy as well.

At Mass today, place any fears you might have about Jesus' judgment into his loving, merciful hands. Remember that each day is a fresh start to "aspire to please" him in all things (2 Corinthians 5:9). Jesus is a judge, yes, but the most kind and merciful judge you will ever encounter!

*"Jesus, I thank you for the mercy you show me each day."*

▶ **Ezekiel 17:22-24**
**Psalm 92:2-3, 13-16**
**Mark 4:26-34**

# 13

**Sunday, June 13**
**2 Corinthians 5:6-10**

*We must all appear before the judgment seat of Christ.*
(2 Corinthians 5:10)

The thought of appearing before the judgment seat of Christ at the end of our lives is, at best, unsettling. That's because we will receive recompense for what we have done, "whether good or evil"

Second, while we may find it painful to remember some of our past sins and misdeeds, Jesus views our lives very differently. He won't see only our sins; he'll also see our good deeds—even the ones we weren't aware of. You may be surprised by the effects that your love has had on the people around you!

Finally, while we're still here on earth, we shouldn't burden ourselves worrying about whether we have done enough good works to earn a spot in heaven. Jesus has already saved us through his "one righteous act"—the shedding of his blood on the cross (Romans 5:18).

## 12 Saturday, June 12
### The Immaculate Heart of Mary

### Luke 2:41-51

*His mother kept all these things in her heart.* (Luke 2:51)

Today's Gospel reading makes it clear that whatever the Immaculate Heart of Mary means, it doesn't mean that Mary was serene and untroubled. It doesn't mean that she was devoid of questions about what God was asking of her and how her son's special vocation was to unfold. Her question here even sounds like a reproach: *Why have you done this to us? We have been very worried* it about Jesus' relationship with his heavenly Father that would move him—a mere youth—to abandon his parents and spend three days in a big city by himself? Only when Jesus began his public ministry could Mary begin to find answers to questions like these.

What does it mean to ponder? It means to sit quietly with our thoughts—and with the Lord. It may also involve a bit of reading to help bolster our understanding or a conversation with a wise friend. This kind of pondering will help us when we want to bring our own reproaches before the Lord. Rather

# CRIME AND PUNISHMENT

## CHARACTER ANALYSES

### Luzhin

While there is a certain grandeur in Svidrigaylov's evildoings, Luzhin is merely despicable. Vain and vindictive, he cloaks his true character with a veneer of respectability. He is the modern version of the Scribes and the Pharisees of the New Testament whose external behavior was above reproach but whose spirit was corrupt. His vanity is especially apparent in one of the conversations with Lebeziatnikov during the course of which the latter mistakenly praises him for being willing to contribute to the establishment of a commune and for being so liberal as to allow Dunya to take a lover after marriage, Luzhin so enjoys the flattery that he accepts praise for virtues that are anathema to him. The man's vindictiveness is brought out in the way he attempts to revenge himself on Raskolnikov. First, he tries to drive a wedge between the student and his family by misrepresenting the young man's relationship to Sonia. When this is unsuccessful, he devises the scheme to falsely accuse Sonia of stealing money from him. Moreover, he has all the makings of a tyrant. As we know, he wants to marry Dunya because her poverty will allow him to enslave her.

Dostoevsky vents his full hatred on Luzhin because he represents everything the author despised in a human being: pettiness and hypocrisy. Such men pretend to uphold the law and claim to believe in fair play, but lie and cheat if some personal benefit can be derived from it. With a clear conscience the Luzhins of the world trample underfoot the very rights they profess to uphold, laud behavior and values in which they do not believe, and look upon misery with indifference.

## The Marmeladovs

This family is a psychological study of the effects of poverty on human dignity. Both the husband and wife lose their self-respect as they sink deeper and deeper into poverty. When the widowed Katerina Ivanovna marries Marmeladov, she is filled with self-pity that economic necessity has forced her to marry below her station. She compensates for her position by constantly reminding her husband of her high position in society. Denied her respect, Marmeladov gets her attention by becoming an alcoholic. Peculiar as it may seem, he positively enjoys having his wife box his ears and pull him about by the hair after his drinking bouts. Because of her, he finds perverse pleasure in his degradation.

As the reader soon discovers, Katerina does not nag her husband because he is of inferior birth, or because she holds him responsible for her predicament. It is her way of compensating. She clings to her upper-class background because it is the symbol of her self-respect. Her past is the one thing that distinguishes her from the lower-class people with whom she is forced to live. Significantly, the further her family declines, the more unrealistic the fantasies become until, shortly before her death, she imagines that she and Sonia will return to the provinces to establish a boarding school for the children of aristocrats. The obsession with her past reaches the point where, at the funeral dinner, she can no longer communicate with people.

There is evidence, too, that she wants to die so as to "punish" society for permitting her this fate. She aggravates her cough on purpose by refusing to open the windows or shut the door although the most unhealthy air wafts in from the other apartments. She stays up late working despite her exhaustion, screams at the slightest provocation bring up blood, and then shows the stained handkerchief to anyone who happens to be near.

## Porfiry Petrovich

In recent years the term "law and order" has taken on a negative **connotation**. The phrase evokes images of politicians hypocritically proclaiming the virtues of obedience while they nonchalantly break the law. Porfiry represents the positive side of law and order. He believes that society needs an ordering force to preserve it from itself. For him, laws are not procrustean rules of conduct handed down arbitrarily by indifferent despots but merely the legalistic formulations of traditional moral values. Dostoevsky makes him the symbol of order and enlightenment. Accordingly, the office where he receives Raskolnikov is clean, bright with sunshine, and furnished with light colored, comfortable chairs. The detective himself is always well groomed and properly dressed. Raskolnikov, the symbol of revolt, lives in a cramped cubicle under the eaves. Like his ideas, the room is dark and gloomy. His clothes are scarcely more than rags, and he practices little, if any, personal hygiene. The difference between the two men is also brought out by the way they express themselves. Speaking in measured, complete sentences. Porfiry develops his ideas carefully. The student's conversation, by comparison, often consists of non-sequiturs. He is rarely able to concentrate for more than a few moments at a time or think an idea through to its end.

Porfiry bears no resemblance to the stereotyped image of a detective. Somewhat overweight, he strikes the reader as faintly comical. Nor does he pursue his victim in the traditional way. Surprisingly adept at psychology, he understands the effect that breaking the law has upon the human mind. Crime is more than just overstepping a regulation. It means to put oneself outside the community, to alienate oneself from his fellow human beings. Porfiry also knows that the isolated individual's first concern is to rejoin the community. Consequently, his technique consists in the simple tactic of letting the criminal incriminate himself. He does this by depriving the suspect of a firm basis or "definite position." A criminal is beyond the reach of the police so long as he knows where he stands. If he is aware, for example, that he is not suspected, he will appear self-confident. And, too, if he is accused of the crime or locked up, he knows where he stands and can consider the best way of defending himself. But what a person is least capable of enduring is uncertainty. If Porfiry merely hints that the man is suspected then, like the moth and the candle, the guilty party will turn up where he is not wanted, speak when he should keep silent, and end by incriminating himself.

Finally, the visit to Raskolnikov reveals Porfiry's deep concern for humanity. He has no interest in catching the student so as to add another solved case to his record. He wants to help the young man by telling him what he must do to regain his self-respect. It is, of course, Dostoevsky speaking when the detective says the crimes can be expiated only by suffering the punishment that society prescribes.

## Raskolnikov

Young, talented, and ambitious, Raskolnikov would have been destined for great things were he born into more favorable circumstances. As it is, all that society permits him is a miserable room to live in and rags for clothes. Add to this hunger and constant worry about his future and it is understandable that the murder of the pawnbroker becomes an acceptable solution for him.

Just when the reader begins to sympathize with the student's reasons, however, the superman theory is introduced. Now the crime is justified from a different angle. Men of superior spirit, so we are told, may kill with impunity whenever they see fit and with amazement we see that Raskolnikov claims to be one of them.

Despite his intelligence, Raskolnikov is a confused young man. He does not know who he is nor what he wants. He insults friends and enemies alike and the only important thing to him through much of the novel is to prove his ideas right.

If we reject his way of thinking, why does he have our sympathy? It is because we understand that his theory is the only thing that gives him hope and self-respect in his otherwise degraded social position. As Sonia is buoyed up by God, Katerina Ivanovna by her upper-class - "one may say aristocratic" -background, so Raskolnikov is sustained by believing himself a person of superior spirit. The danger in organizing one's life around such illusions is that when the false belief collapses, the person is left drifting in a void. Hence, the murder threatens to destroy Raskolnikov because the archetypal guilt feeling that immediately engulfs him after the crime makes him almost forget the theory that sustained him over the last months. Still, he can regain life, hope, by voluntarily submitting himself to the punishment prescribed by one's culture. More than any other character, Raskolnikov embodies the author's conviction that man is not an island, that by his very nature the individual is a creature who cannot endure alienation from the human community.

## Razumikhin

This man stands out in sharp relief to most of the characters in Dostoevsky's gallery of tortured seekers. Tall and clean-cut, he has accepted himself for what he is, knows what he wants, and does not expect more from life than he is prepared to give. He is not bitter for having been forced to withdraw from the university for lack of funds. Instead he starts to work, planning to resume his studies as soon as possible. Above all, he has learned the simple lesson that to preserve peace of mind in a world characterized by banality and injustice, one must not take life too seriously or view one's position in it as tragic. This attitude enables him to live in the world and conform to its requirements without losing his self-respect.

## Sonia

Though forced into prostitution to save her family, Sonia remains childlike and innocent. The source of her strength is implicit faith in God. Not God the reward giver, but God the dispenser of divine justice. Thus, it is inconceivable for her that He will refuse to provide for her brother and sisters or that He will allow her no other fate than prostitution. Dostoevsky proves her right in that not only are the children rescued but at the end she is also saved.

Sonia represents Dostoevsky's idea that spiritual rebirth is earned through suffering. It is worth noting that the name Sonia is the diminutive form of her real name, Sophia. In Russian religious thought the concept of Sophia (wisdom) takes on the added meaning of universal love. Through Sophia one can penetrate to the divine essence of things and enter into communion with what is there. It is a kind of joining of man, God, and nature. Sonia embodies this concept. She understands that everything exists in and through God. Her chief function in the novel is to lead Raskolnikov to this recognition. As the symbol of rebirth in faith, she stands out in sharp relief to Svidrigaylov who has forfeited all hope for redemption.

## Svidrigaylov

This man illustrates Dostoevsky's conviction that a person who has no religion - whether it be belief in God, humanity, his native land, or any other cause outside his own personal interests - will stagnate. Believing in and wanting nothing, he wastes his life listlessly passing from one experience to another. No thought or activity brings the intense exhilaration for which he thirsts. Since he has no real concept of good and evil in the religious or philosophical sense, he can do virtually anything he wants. Most of the time he has no desire for anything because he regards everything as one and the same. This **metaphysical** boredom is the price Svidrigaylov pays for his freedom. Indifferent to Christianity and so unable to believe in a Hereafter, his philosophy of purposelessness manifests itself even in his view of eternity as a one room bath house in the country.

Thus Svidrigaylov shows what awaits the person who organizes his life around the principle that all things are permissible. Freedom from a higher principle means eternal boredom. At the end, nothing is left but suicide.

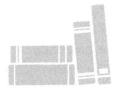

# CRIME AND PUNISHMENT

## ESSAY QUESTIONS AND ANSWERS

. . . . . . . . . . . . . . . . . . . . . . . . . . . . . . . . . . . . . . . . . . . . . . . . . . . . . . . . . .

Question: What is the function of Raskolnikov's dreams?

Answer: On the psychological level, the dreams act as a kind of catharsis in which the dominant idea is manifested in a new and violent form. It is noteworthy that immediately preceding each dream the hero is in a state of disease and delirium, often bordering on madness. Furthermore, the dreams are an unconscious attempt to shift responsibility for the violence, as if Raskolnikov in his conscious state were incapable of such actions.

The first dream of the mare beating shows that while one side of Raskolnikov - the child - is appalled at the brutality, another part of him - the murderer - identifies with the cruelty. Like the horse's owner, the student will take an axe and kill. Significantly, immediately after awakening Raskolnikov marvels that he is actually capable of murder.

His second dream of the dead Alyona mocking his futile efforts to kill her suggests his own impotence and by extension the invalidity of his theory. After this dream, he realizes once and for all that he is the true victim of the crime because in killing the old woman he destroyed the principle around which his life was organized.

The final dream of the plague expresses a new way of looking at the fundamental error of Raskolnikov's life. The new strain of microbes that destroy humanity is merely a symbol of a malady already afflicting the world, the lack of faith and commitment. Men struck by the disease are characterized by a sense of purposelessness. All that remains is reason and self-will which, devoid of a guiding principle, turn back upon and destroy themselves. The dream also embodies the means for Raskolnikov's spiritual regeneration. He must focus his strength and will upon a humanistic, Christian ideal. This dream marks the beginning of Raskolnikov's new life.

Question: What is Dostoevsky's attitude toward reason?

Answer: Dostoevsky distrusts rationalism as too far removed from reality. He holds feeling in higher esteem because he believes that only through feeling can we know the totality of any experience. Feeling transcends the limitations imposed by reason. In a letter to his brother Michael, October 31, 1838 he wrote: "Nature, the soul, love, and God one recognizes through the heart, and not through reason...But when our aim is the understanding of love or of nature, we march toward the very citadel of the heart... Philosophy cannot be regarded as a mere equation where nature is the unknown quantity."

There is a similar statement in *Notes from Underground*. The Underground Man claims that man does not consistently act as his reason and advantage dictate because the assumption that man is a rational creature is simply not valid. He rejects reason because it represents only one side of man's being. The explanation for this attitude is not far to seek. He disagrees with certain thinkers who claim the existence of laws governing human behavior much like those governing the physical universe. If such laws exist, man can eventually set up tables of behavior predictive of every human action as he has done for mathematics. But the Underground Man rejects the laws of human nature and says that man is free to create his own law. He maintains that there is no a priori good and evil in his world. Man does not choose what is already determined, rather all human actions are devoid of value until their value is determined at the moment of choice. This way of looking at ethics illustrates Dostoevsky's belief in man's basic goodness. As long as the individual makes feeling the basis of his ethical behavior, in most cases good will result.

Question: Does Raskolnikov want to get caught and be punished, or to stay free and go unpunished?

Answer: There is considerable evidence to support the view that Raskolnikov wants his theory proved wrong, get caught, and be punished. The first indication appears in his preparation for the crime. It is by no means meticulous. To be sure, he has gotten the false pledge ready, rehearsed the crime, counted the steps to Alyona's house and even devised a noose to carry the axe. Yet as incredible as it may seem, he has made only the most elementary plans for securing the axe and getting it back unseen. Everything rests upon Nastasya's absence from the kitchen at the precise moment he needs it. Furthermore, he tries to sabotage his plans by taking a nap and oversleeping the time he knows Alyona to be alone. Then he does not remember to get rid of his stove-pipe hat. When he remembers the mistake, he leaves it on anyway.

Again, Raskolnikov is guilty of incredible oversights following the murder. First he forgets to lock the door and is forced to kill

Lizaveta who walks in. Next, with the door still open, he dallies several minutes washing the axe, then he scrutinizes his clothes for traces of blood, all seemingly in the unconscious hope that someone will arrive while he is still there.

So Raskolnikov appears to be running toward punishment rather than away from it. He returns to his room, pockets bulging with stolen articles, and falls asleep, forgetting to lock the door. From here on he is continually putting out clues to encourage suspicion. The day after the murder he answers a summons to the police which he expects deals with the murder. When he discovers that he is not suspected, he faints to incur suspicion. Then he almost confesses to Zametov in the tavern and later, while visiting the scene of the crime, he gives the men working there his name and address. He also encourages Porfiry's pursuit by seeking him out and provoking his suspicions. Significantly, when Porfiry visits him in his room and declares that he has no evidence which could convict him, the author says that: "The thought that Porfiry thought him innocent began to frighten him suddenly." At last, when there are neither clues nor people who can incriminate him, he confesses.

There is little argument among critics that Raskolnikov wants to get caught. Disagreement revolves around his reasons. Some insist that it is simply a matter of the criminal's realization that he has broken the law. That after recognizing his mistake, he seeks the punishment. All his actions can be attributed to a desire to return to human society. An opposing view claims that the student needs the punishment to prove his strength and his right to crime. Yet, Raskolnikov can sustain his belief in the superman theory only as long as his conception of society as a mass of automatons is unimpaired. After killing the old woman, he slowly begins to realize that his ideas smack of oversimplification. Although he tries to hold onto them, he senses that if the death of a "louse" can affect him so severely, there must be more to life and the human condition than a neatly thought out theory. He does not know what it is but intuitively feels that by suffering punishment he may discover it. At the end of the novel Sonia points the way.

# BIBLIOGRAPHY

......................................................

## I. BOOK CRITICISM AND BIOGRAPHY

What follows is a list of books containing material on *Crime and Punishment*. They have been selected on the basis of usefulness to the student. The books starred are available in paperback.

Berdyaev, Nicholas. *Dostoevsky.* New York: Meridian, 1957. Berdyaev's book takes a philosophical approach to Dostoevsky's novel. In the chapter "Evil" the author gives particular attention to *Crime and Punishment*, and to Raskolnikov's theory of the extraordinary man. On the whole, this book is an adequate introduction to Dostoevsky's ideas.

Curle, Richard. *Characters of Dostoevsky. Studies from Four Novels.* London: William Heinemann Ltd., 1950. The major characters of *Crime and Punishment* are individually discussed in this work. The profiles are not distinguished by their depth of insight, but they are helpful in pointing out the characters' salient features.

Fueloep-Miller, René. *Fyodor Dostoevsky. Insight, Faith, and Prophecy.* New York: Charles Scribner's Sons, 1950. Of particular interest to the student concerned with the role of dreams in *Crime and Punishment* is the chapter entitled

"Dostoevsky—A Forerunner of Psychoanalysis." The author, for example, analyzes the dream in which Raskolnikov strikes the dead pawnbroker as the young man's subconscious admission of the failure of his theories. In another interesting chapter, "Dostoevsky's Prophecies," Fueloep-Miller discusses the practical realization of Raskolnikov's theories in contemporary history.

Gide, André. *Dostoevsky*. New York: New Directions, 1961. This book is in part
made up of lectures written at a time in France (in the early 1920's) when
Dostoevsky was not widely read or appreciated. Gide's book sets out to
evaluate and to establish Dostoevsky's place among the great writers
of the world. The author deals with several of Dostoevsky's novels in a
general fashion. This book should be read for Gide's brilliant insights into
the pattern of Dostoevsky's themes; much of the material on Dostoevsky's
life however, has been superseded by more recent biographies.

Ivanov, Vyacheslav. *Freedom and the Tragic Life: A Study in Dostoevsky*.
New York: The Noonday Press, 1960. Ivanov's book emphasizes
Dostoyoevsky's philosophical and theological views. Particular attention
is given to *Crime and Punishment* in his chapter "The Revolt Against
Mother Earth." Ivanov discusses Dostoevsky's idea of salvation through
suffering.

Lavrin, Janko. *Dostoevsky: A Study*. New York: The Macmillan Company, 1947.
Lavrin's book investigates Dostoevsky the artist and the psychologist.
In the chapter "The Bankruptcy of the Superman" Lavrin examines
Raskolnikov's superman theories.

Murry, John Middleton. *Fyodor Dostoevsky: A Critical Study*. London: Martin
Secker, 1923.

Powys, John Cowper. *Dostoevsky: A Study*. London: Lane, 1946.

Roe, Ivan. *The Breath of Corruption: An Interpretation of Dostoevsky*. London: Hutchinson, 1946.

Simmons, Ernest J. *Dostoevsky: The Making of a Novelist*. Oxford University Press, 1940.

Steiner, George. *\*Tolstoy or Dostoevsky: An Essay in the Old Criticism*. New York: Vintage Books, 1959. Steiner's book contains brilliant insights into Dostoevsky's symbolism, and relates Dostoevsky's writings to other world masterpieces.

Yarmolinsky. Avrahm. *\*Dostoevsky: His Life and Art*. New York: Grove Press, Inc., 1960. Yarmolinsky's book is an energetic and vivid account of Dostoevsky's life. The chapter "A Russian Tragedy" deals with *Crime and Punishment*. For anyone interested in Dostoevsky's life at the time of his writing the novel, this chapter is essential. Moreover, the author offers sound observations on the characters and themes in the novel.

## II. ESSAYS AND ARTICLES

For the student writing a paper on *Crime and Punishment*, or for the reader interested in exploring the novel in depth, the following material is indispensable.

## A. Collections of Essays

Blackmur, R. P. "*Crime and Punishment: A Study of Dostoevsky*." Essays in Modern Literary Criticism. (edited by Ray B. West), New York: Rinehart, 1952.

Rahv, Philip. "Dostoevsky in *Crime and Punishment*." *\*Dostoevsky: A Collection of Critical Essays* (edited by René Wellek), Englewood Cliffs,

N. J.: Prentice Hall, Inc., 1962. This is undoubtedly the best selection of essays on Dostoevsky contained in one book. There is an international representation of critics who examine the entire spectrum of Dostoevsky's novels and ideas. Mr. Rahv's article in this collection touches upon almost every important aspect of the novel. What the essay has in breadth of examination it also contains in depth of analysis. Any abstract of its contents must be superficial since every line of the article is informative and insightful. His discussion, for example, dwells upon such subjects as Svidrigailov's sexual nihilism; Dostoevsky's attitude toward violence; and the significance of Raskolnikov's dreams.

Wasiolek, Edward (Editor). *Crime and Punishment and the Critics*. San Francisco: Wadsworth Publishing Company, 1961.

## B. Articles in Periodicals

Beebe, Maurice. "The Three Motives of Raskolnikov: A Reinterpretation of *Crime and Punishment.*" *College English*, Volume XVII, December 1955. In his well-argued essay Mr. Beebe suggests that Raskolnikov is a masochist, and that he killed the pawnbroker in order to be punished. Raskolnikov's attraction to the landlady's crippled daughter, and his dream of the mare, Mr. Beebe points out, are indications of the young man's aberration. The essay is important for those interested in a psychoanalytic approach to Raskolnikov and his problems.

Dauner, Louise. "Raskolnikov in Search of a Soul." *Modern Fiction Studies*. Volume IV, No. 3, Autumn, 1958. This special issue of the journal is devoted to articles on Dostoevsky. Among the several essays, two deal with *Crime and Punishment*. Of major importance is the magazine's checklist of criticism on Dostoevsky. Miss Dauner's article examines Raskolnikov's psychic maturation in terms of Jung's theories of growth and development. Of particular interest is the discussion of the structural and thematic significance of the number four, which reappears throughout the novel.

Florance, Edna C. "The Neurosis of Raskolnikov: A Study in Incest and Murder." *Archives of Criminal Psychodynamics*, Volume I, 1955.

Gibian, George. "Traditional Symbolism in *Crime and Punishment.*" *Publications of the Modern Language Association of America*, Volume LXX, Number 5, December, 1955. In this excellent article Mr. Gibian investigates the basic symbols in the novel. The critic notes, for example, that water is a death symbol when associated with Svidrigailov, and a death and life symbol when associated with Raskolnikov. Mr. Gibian's pithy article is basic for those interested in the novel's symbolism.

Hoffman, Frederick J. "The Scene of Violence: Dostoevsky and Dreiser." *Modern Fiction Studies*, Volume VI, No. 2, Summer, 1960. Professor Hoffman analyzes the function of environment in *Crime and Punishment* and *An American Tragedy*. He finds that Dreiser's hero, Clyde Griffiths, is manipulated by his environment, and that Raskolnikov wills or shapes his external and internal environment. Although, in the main, the article deals with problems of naturalism, Professor Hoffman also brilliantly explores Raskolnikov's personality and casts much light on a usually overlooked character, Porfiry.

Squires, P. C. "Dostoevsky's Raskolnikov: The Criminalistic Protest." *Journal of Criminal Law*, Volume XXVIII, November, 1937.

Wasiolek, Edward. "On the Structure of *Crime and Punishment.*" *Publications of the Modern Language Association of America*, Volume LXXIV, Number 1, March, 1959. Mr. Wasiolek asserts that too many critics have assumed that *Crime and Punishment* is formless. He demonstrates that the structure of the novel is based upon a balance of opposites. For example, Raskolnikov's rebirth is balanced by Svidrigailov's death. Dostoevsky, the critic maintains, was a conscious artist and able craftsman.

CPSIA information can be obtained
at www.ICGtesting.com
Printed in the USA
BVHW040813010721
610971BV00009B/123